Polly Borland

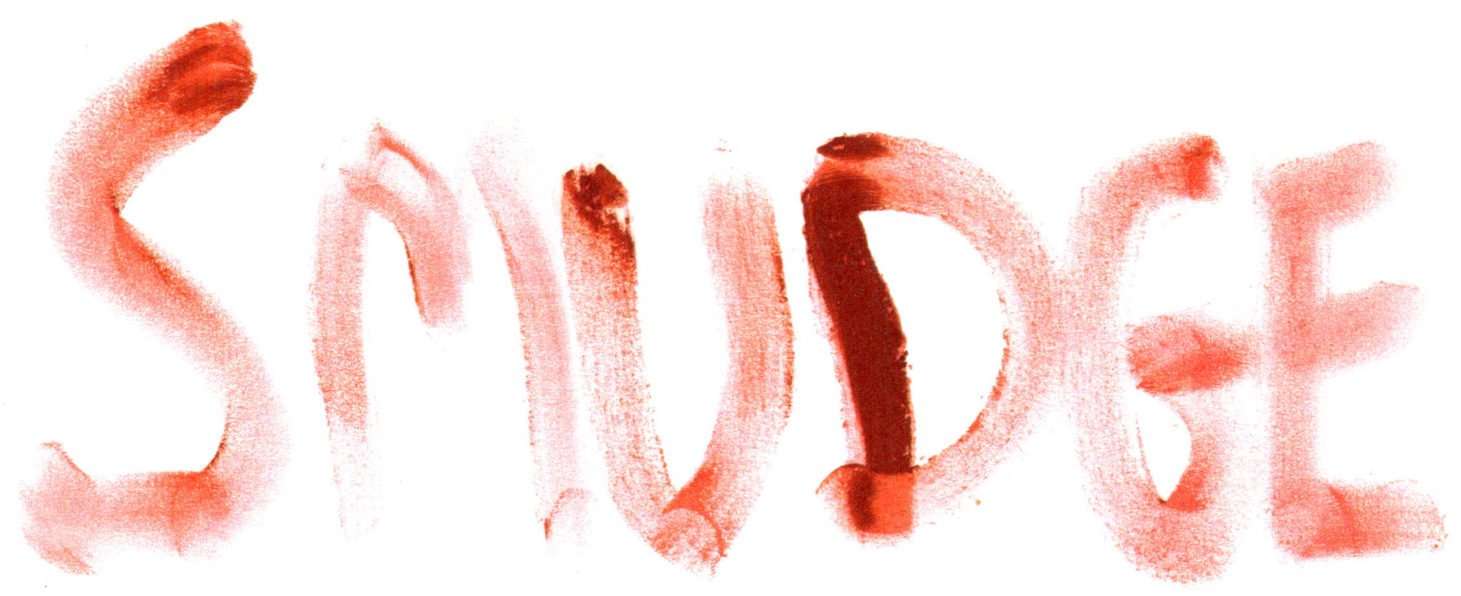
SMUDGE

For my husband John Hillcoat,
son Louie Hillcoat
and sister Emma Borland

Nick Cave

My friend Polly Borland rang one morning. She wanted me to model for some photographs. Now, there are two types of people in this world: those who like having their picture taken and those who don't. I exist squarely in the latter. Polly knows this. So I felt it would come as no surprise to her when I politely refused.

Polly has learnt over the years how to deal with my adversarial relationship with the camera – flattery, bribery, emotional blackmail - but this time her request was different. "I'm not interested in you, darling, just your shape. I need someone *angular*. I want to dress you up. No-one will even know who you are, least of all yourself."

So it was that I went round to her house in Brighton. We played dress ups. Polly squeezed me into body stockings, rubber bathing caps, crotch-accentuating leotards; she shoved ping-pong balls down the front of a lycra tankini, attached cow udders to my face, rouged my nipples, pulled shredded pantyhose over my head; wigs were put on backward – electric blue ones, blonde ones, horrid ones made of rusted steel wool; she glued phallic noses to my forehead, fright-wigged me, squeezed me into glam-rock boob tubes.

"Do I look all right?" I asked through a nylon gag.

"You look beautiful," she replied as she emptied me out, reduced me, objectified me, transposed her crazed and melancholy imaginings onto the little that was left of me. Then with a snap of her camera, Polly ushered me into the community of sad, erotised creatures that populate most of her work. Inside those polyurethane sheaths, those nylon cocoons, I felt pupal and unborn, and so it is with the pictures themselves, the creatures that are revealed are embryonic and ill-formed, in the process of transformation, of coming into being. They are blind, quiescent and yet to be defined, but simultaneously and tragically engaged in the act of dying.

Looking at the photographs now I am moved in the same way I so often am when confronted with Polly's extraordinary photographs. Whether they are the magnificent, life-affirming photographs of the adult baby series, the terrifying erotic distortions of her Bunny pictures or the strange, doomed creatures in these pages, I am struck by Polly's deep love for her subjects and the dignity that exists in their dysmorphia. And it is this that draws us tentatively towards her pictures, the love and the lack of judgement. Because her pictures are never voyeuristic, never observational and never merely shocking. Rather Polly seems to me to be shooting into a distorted mirror and simply bringing back heartbreaking refracted images of herself.

"This is fun!" I cried through a nylon gag.

"You look beautiful," she replied.

Nick Cave

Mi amiga Polly Borland me llamó una mañana. Quería que posara para unas fotografías. Hay dos tipos de personas en el mundo, personas a las que les gusta que les hagan fotos, y personas a las que no. Yo pertenezco al segundo grupo. Polly lo sabe. Así que pensé que no sería una sorpresa para ella si me negaba amablemente.

Polly había aprendido con los años a enfrentarse a mi conflictiva relación con la cámara –halagos, sobornos, chantaje emocional–, pero en esta ocasión pedía algo diferente: "No me interesas tú, querido, sino tu figura. Necesito a alguien "anguloso". Quiero disfrazarte. Nadie, excepto tú, sabrá quién eres".

Así fue que me dejé caer por su casa en Brighton. Y jugamos a disfrazarnos. Polly me puso mallas, gorritos de baño y leotardos marca paquete. Metió bolas de ping-pong en un *tankini* de lycra, me plantó unas ubres de vaca en la cara, me pintó de rojo los pezones y me puso unos pantys rotos en la cabeza. Me puso pelucas al revés: unas de color azul brillante, unas doradas y otras horribles hechas con lana de acero oxidado. Me pegó narices fálicas en la frente y me colocó pelucas extrañas y camisetas-tubo tipo *glam* rock.

"¿Qué tal estoy?" pregunté a través de una mordaza de nailon.

"Estás guapísimo", contestó mientras me vaciaba, me reducía, me despersonalizaba y volcaba sus desbocadas y melancólicas fantasías en lo poco que quedaba de mí. Así, con un clic de su cámara, Polly me introdujo en la comunidad de criaturas tristes y erotizadas que pueblan la mayor parte de su obra. Dentro de esas fundas de poliuretano y esos capullos de nailon me sentí como una crisálida, como un nonato, lo mismo que las propias fotografías: las criaturas de Polly son embrionarias y deformes, en proceso de transformación, de llegar a ser. Están ciegas, inactivas y aún indefinidas, pero se sumen a la vez y de un modo trágico en una agonía cercana a la muerte.

Mirando ahora las fotografías, me emociono como siempre hago cuando me enfrento al resto del extraordinario trabajo de Polly. Ya sean las fotos magníficas y llenas de vida de la serie de bebés adultos, las horripilantes distorsiones eróticas de Bunny, o las extrañas criaturas predestinadas en estas páginas, me conmueve el gran amor de Polly hacia sus modelos y la dignidad que hay en su amorfia. Esto es lo que nos atrae a primera vista de sus fotos: el amor y la ausencia de juicio. Porque sus fotos no son nunca morbosas, ni observacionales, ni meramente escandalosas. Por el contrario, creo que Polly dispara dentro de un espejo distorsionado y, simplemente, obtiene desgarradoras imágenes de sí misma.

"¡Es divertido!" grité a través de una mordaza de nailon.

"You look beautiful", contestó.

All I want to be when I grow up

Polly Borland

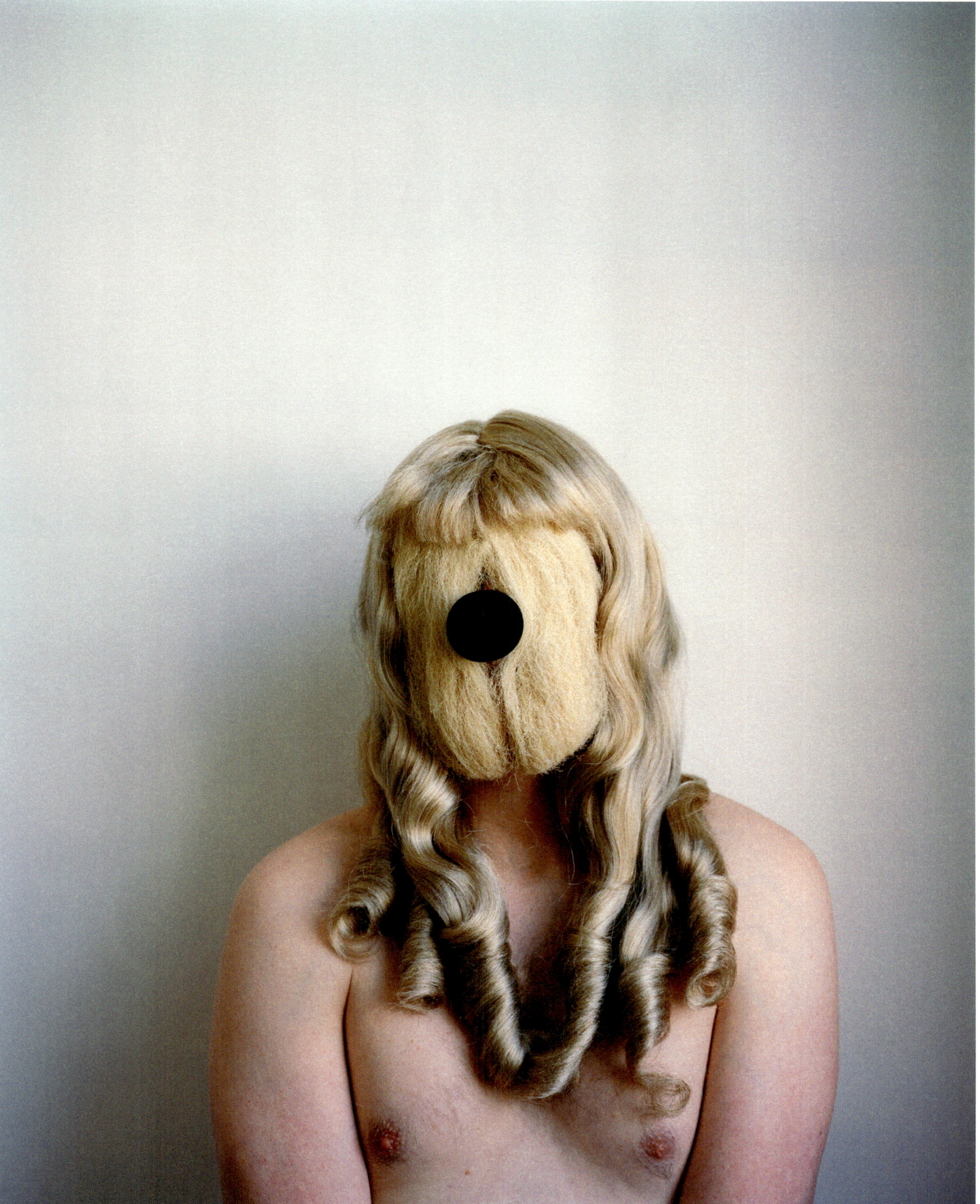

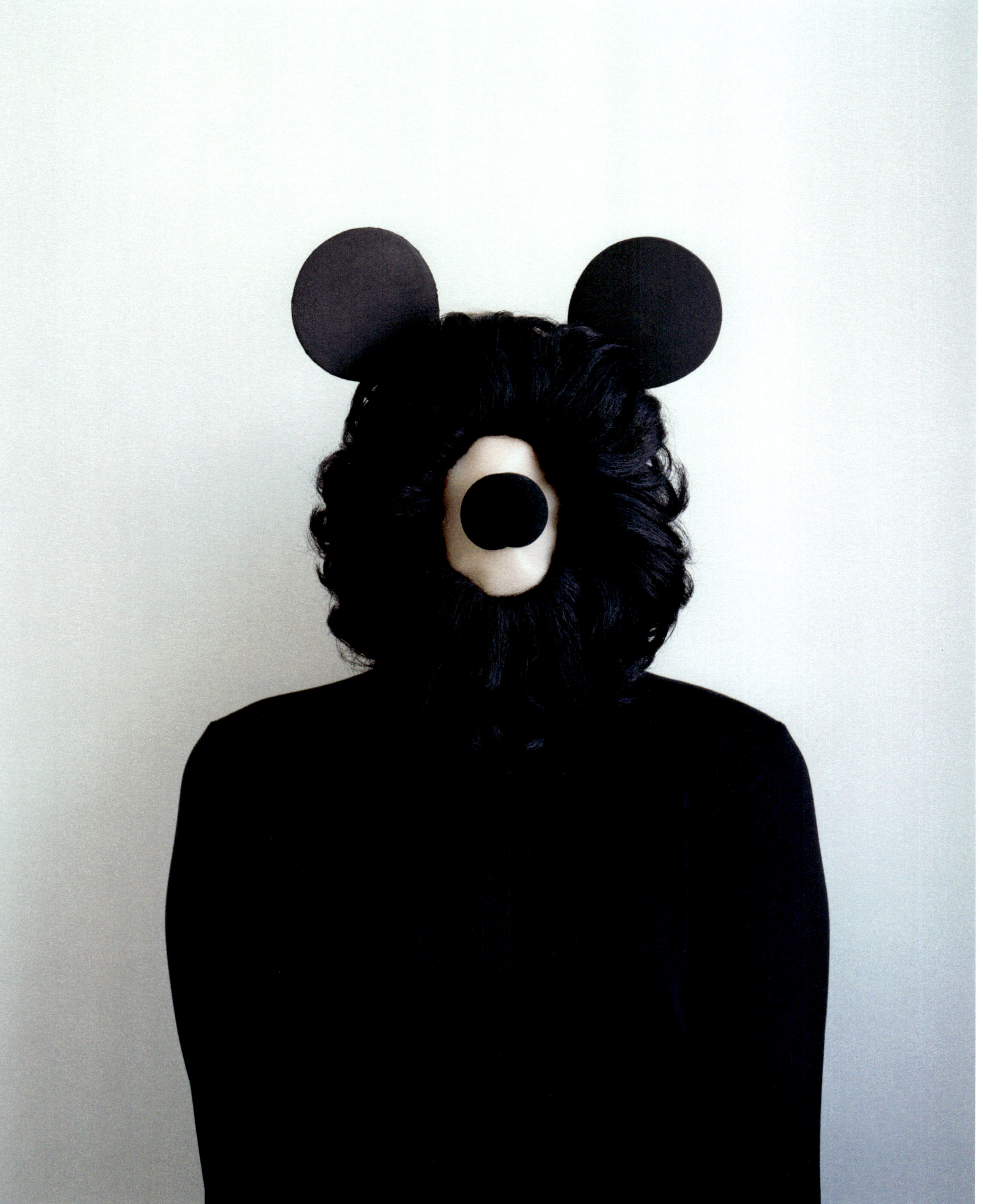

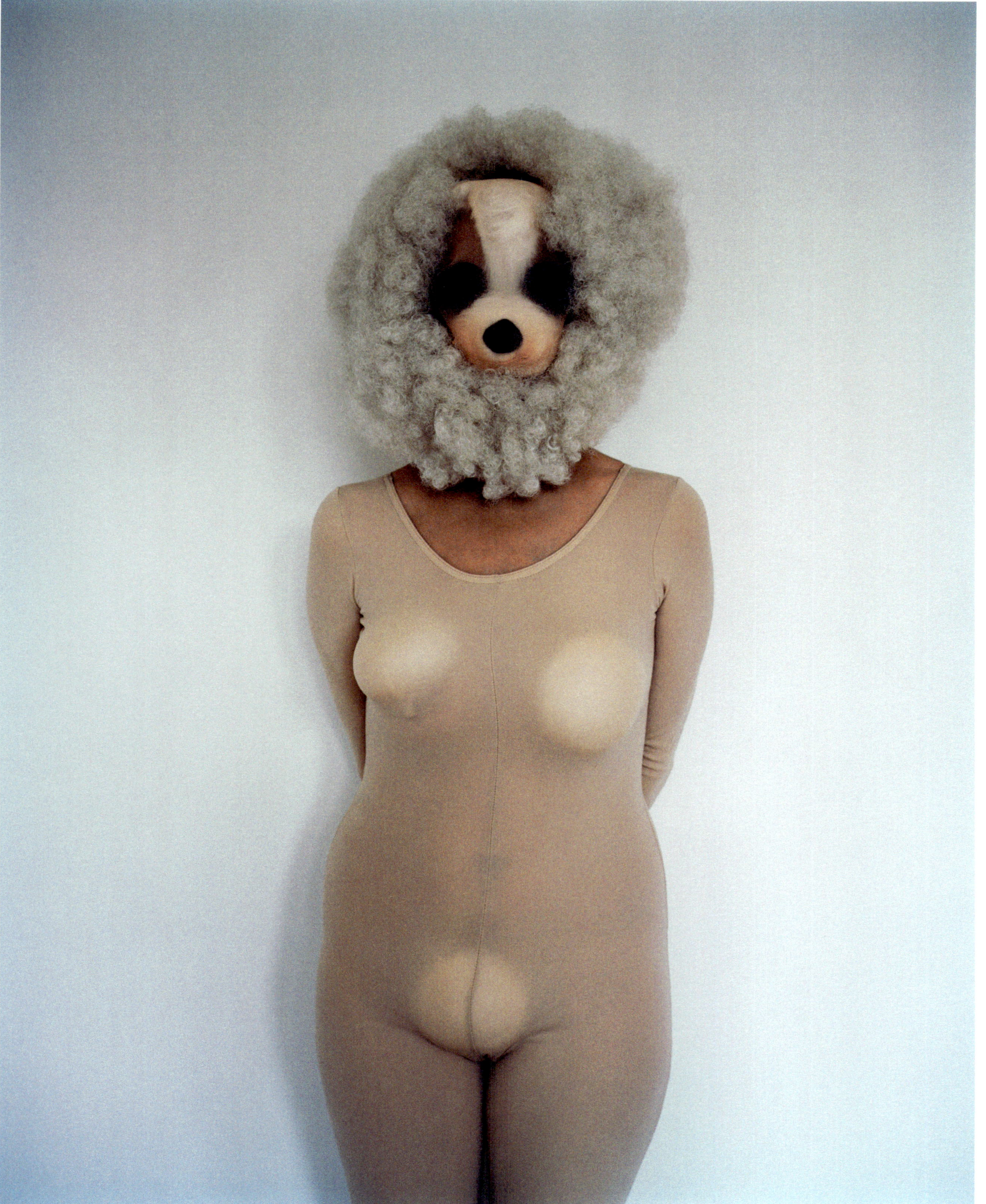

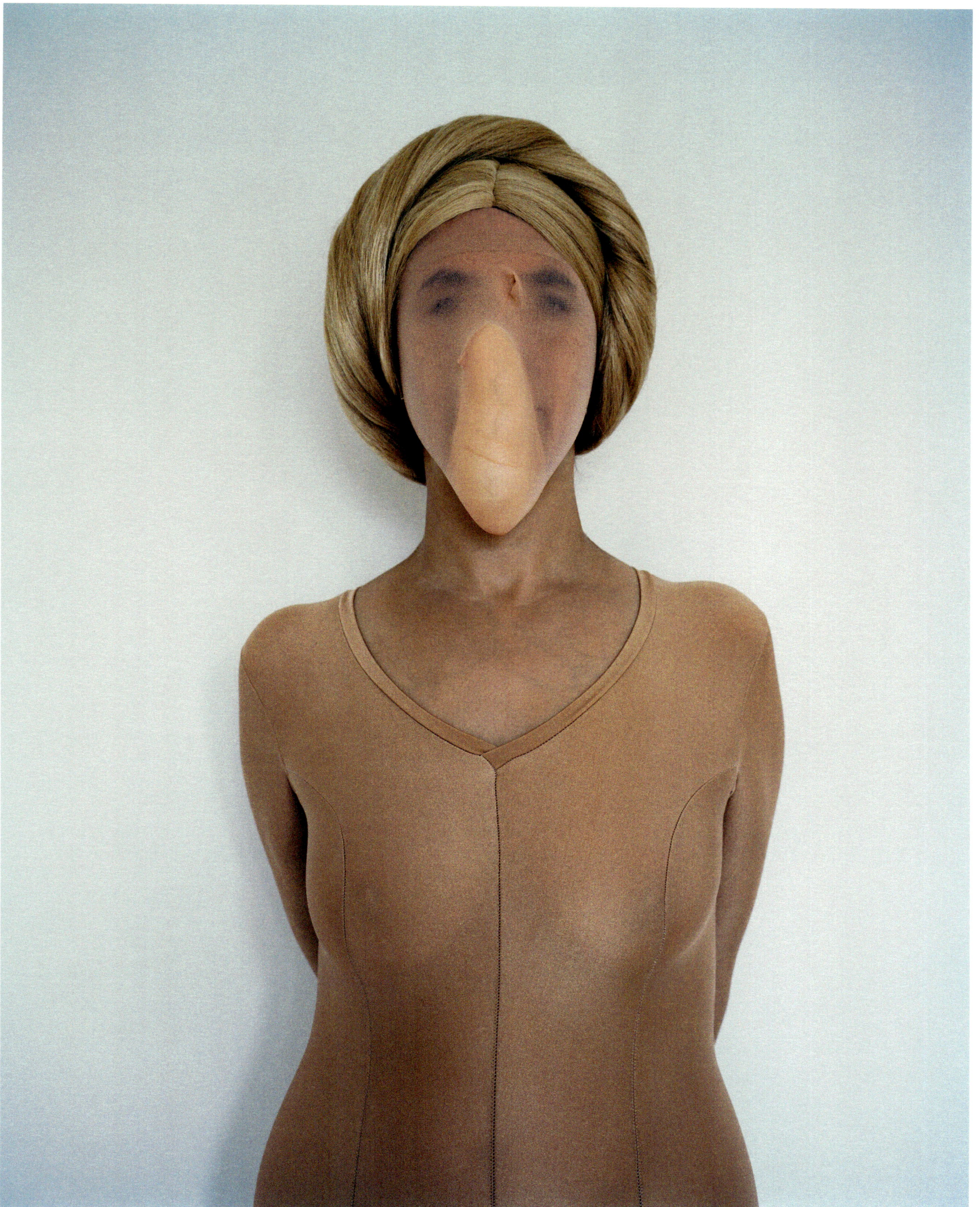

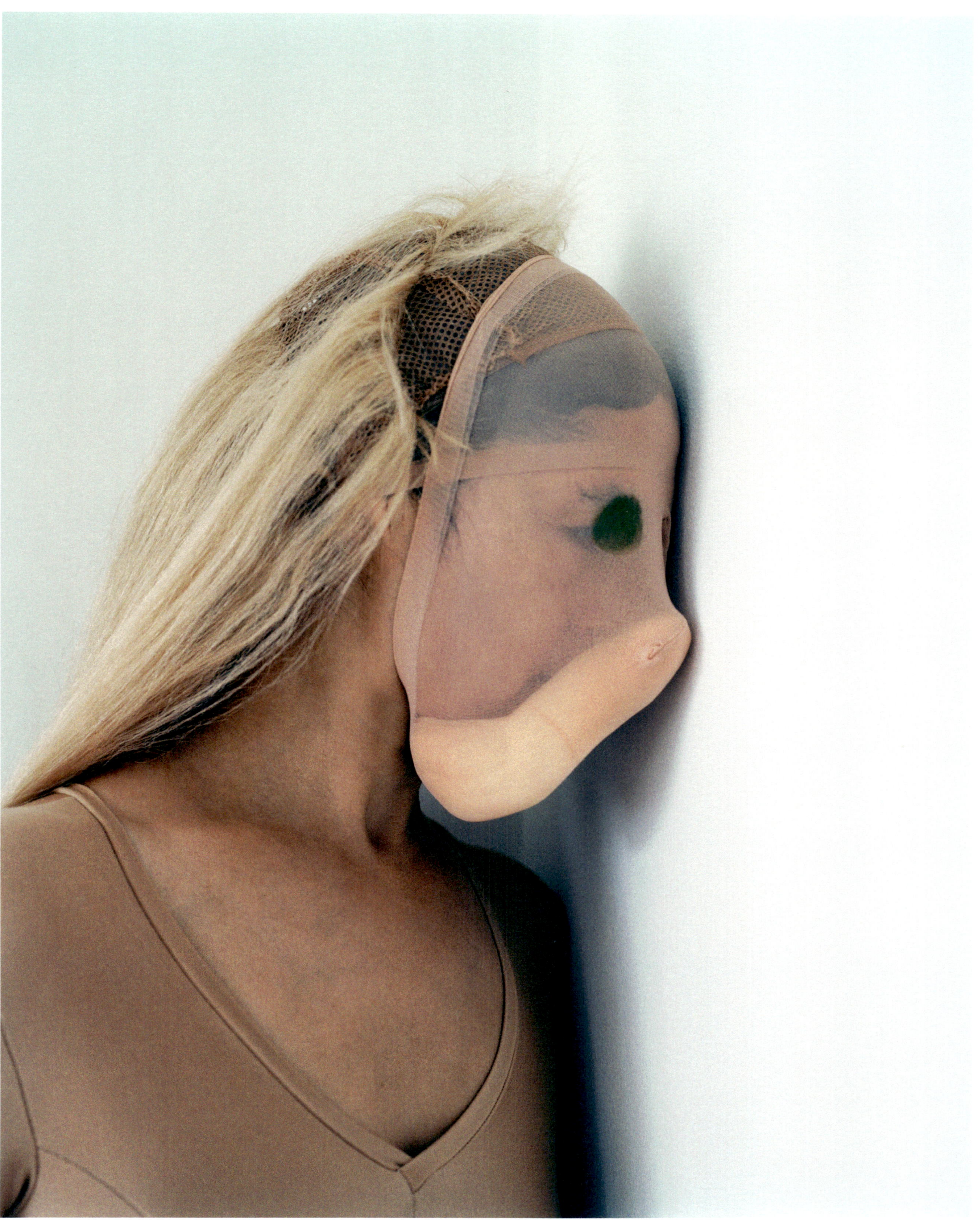

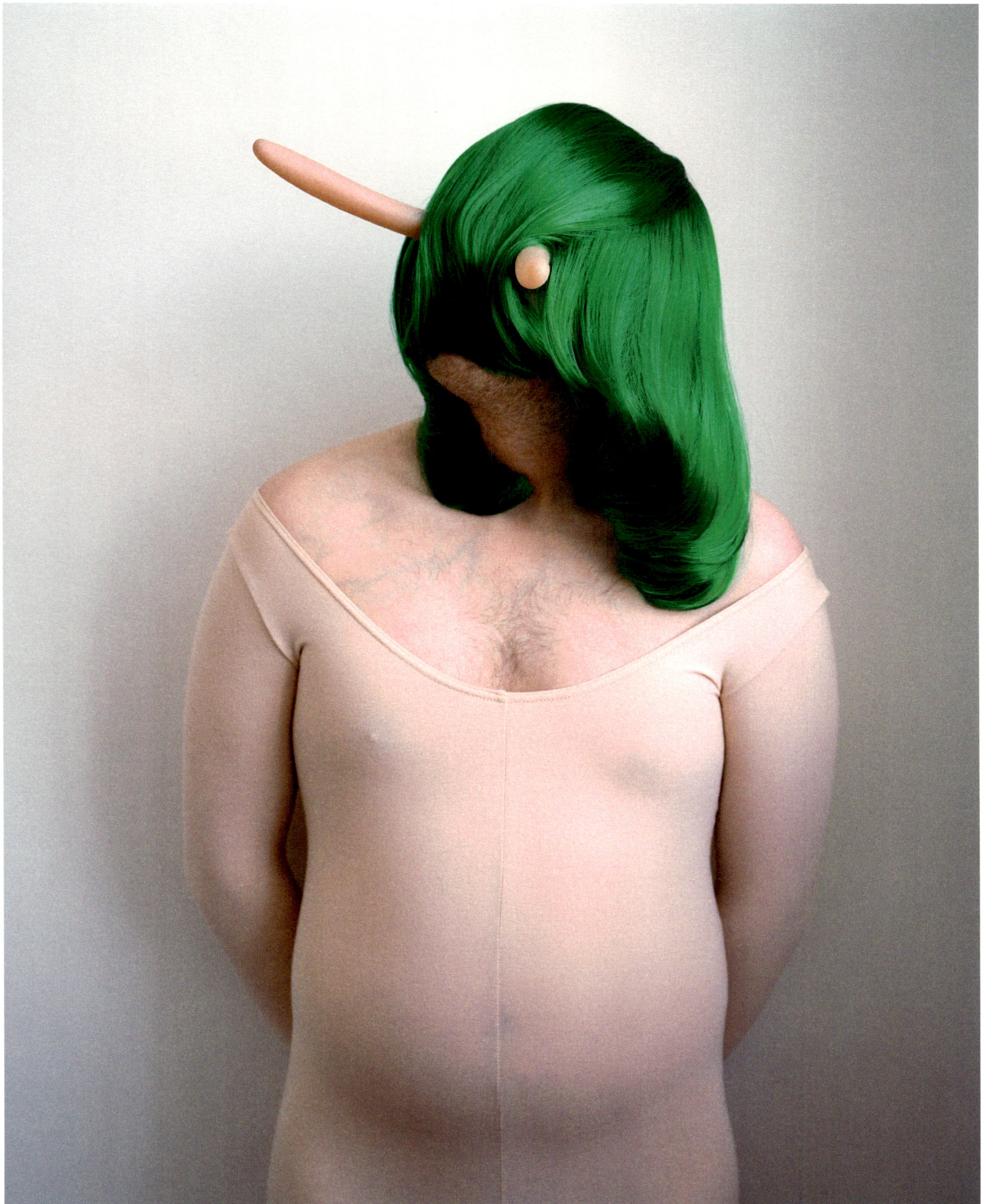

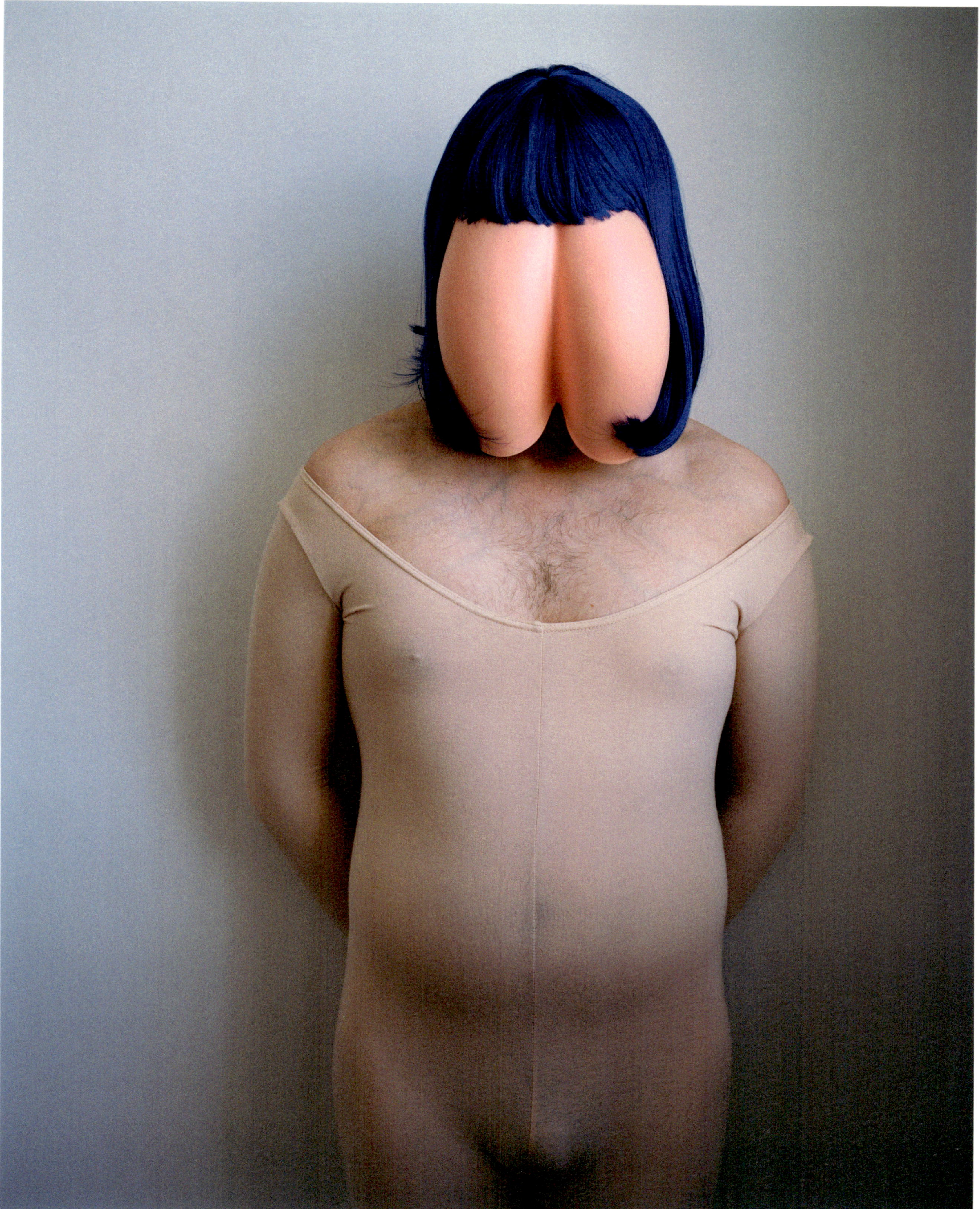

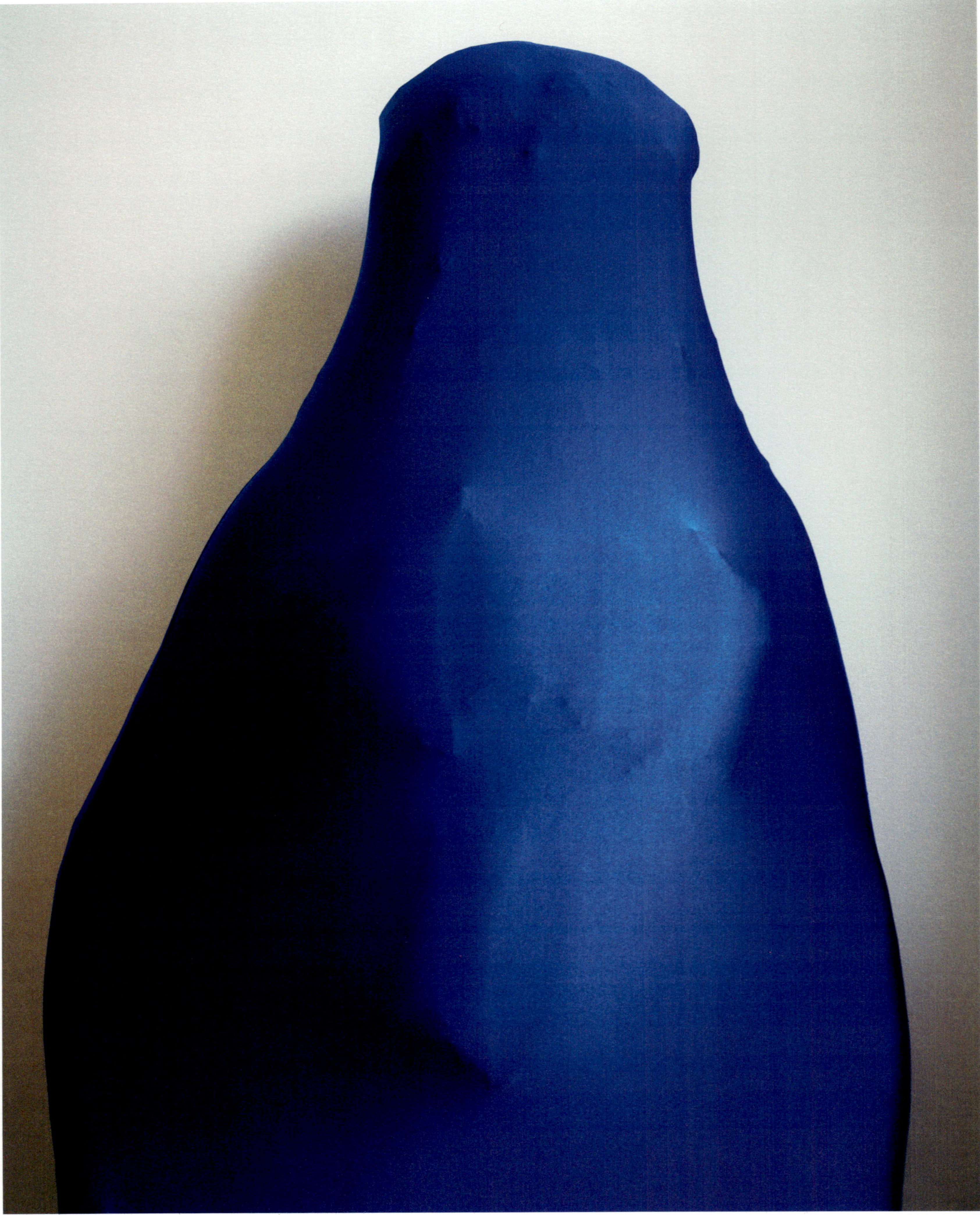

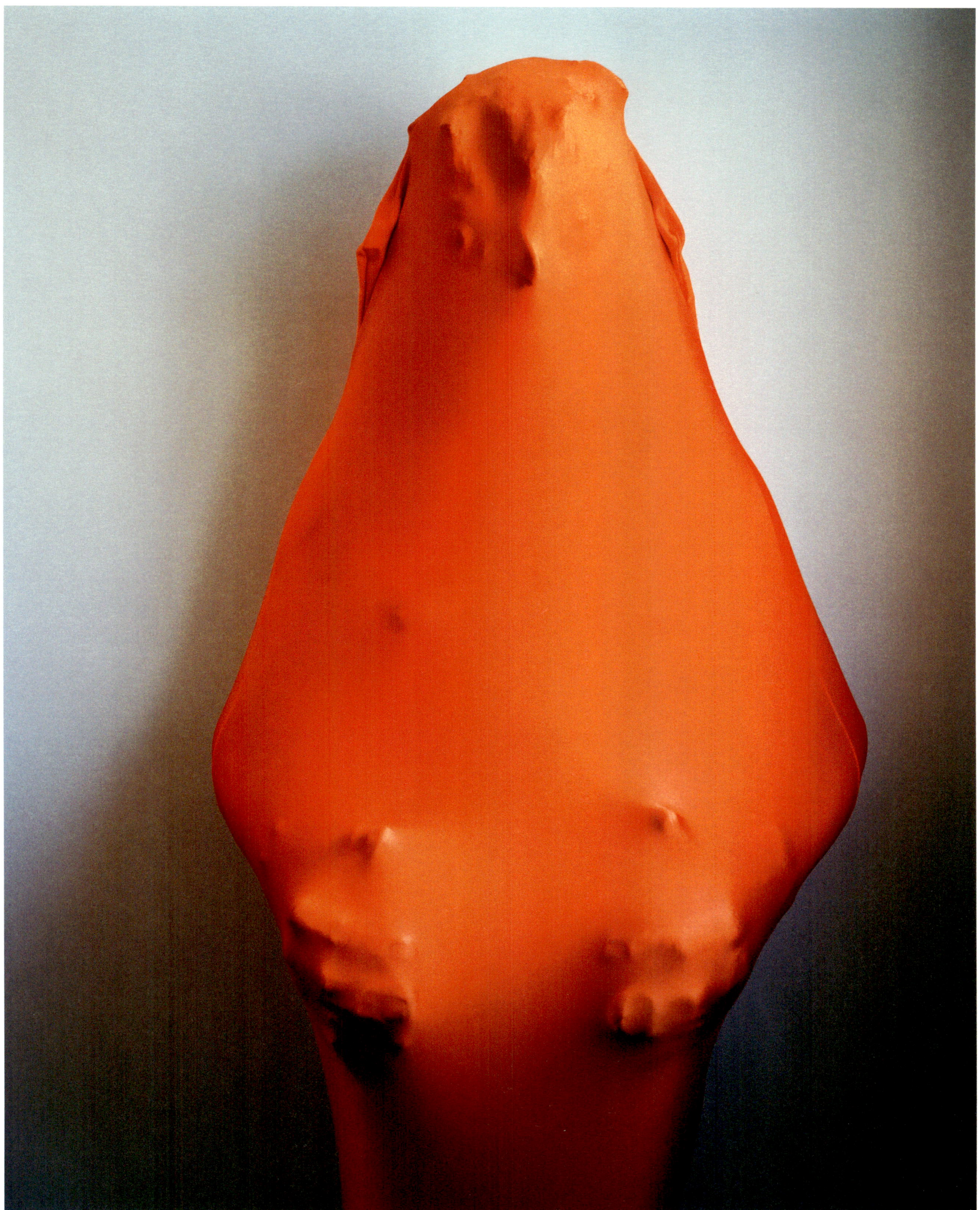

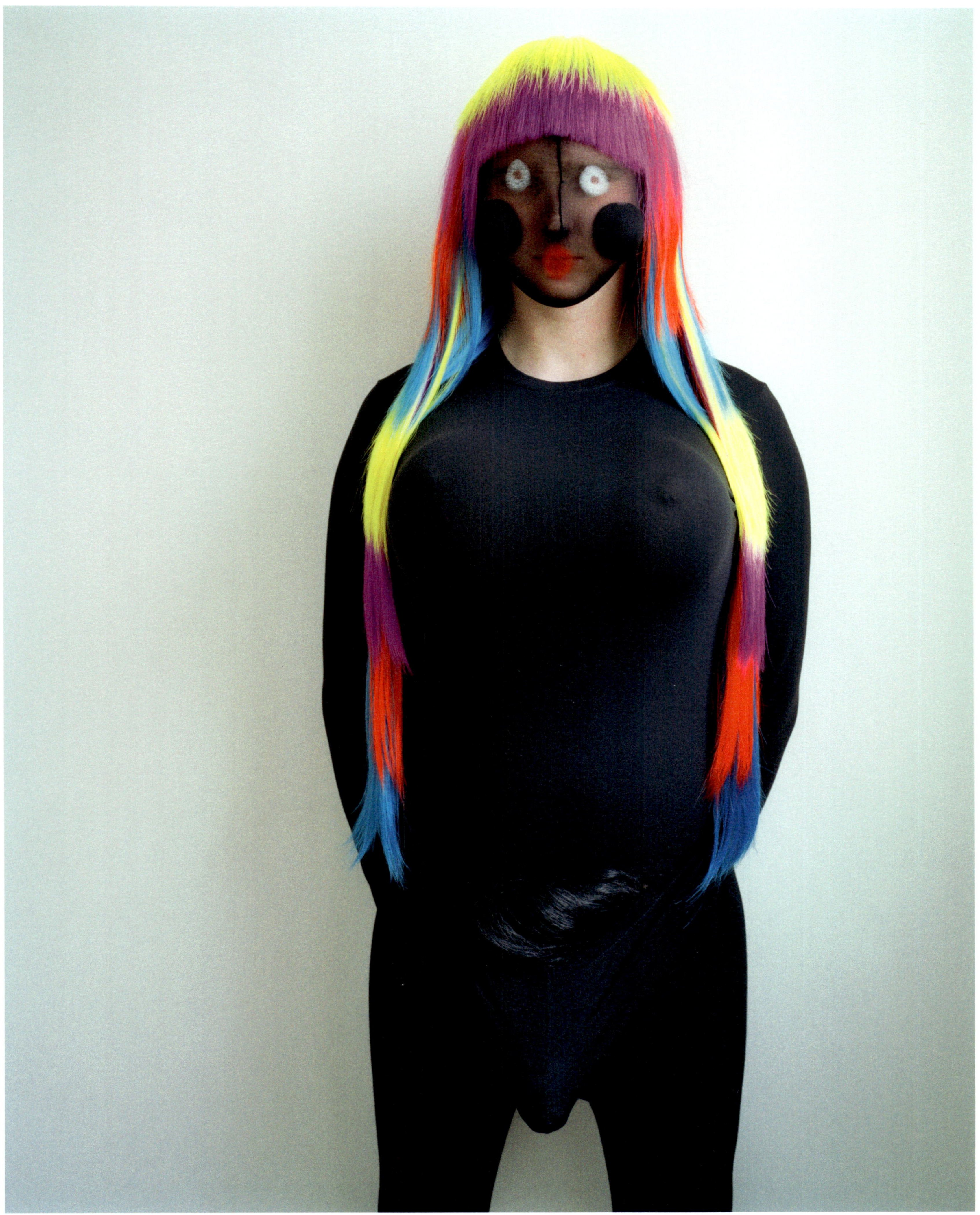

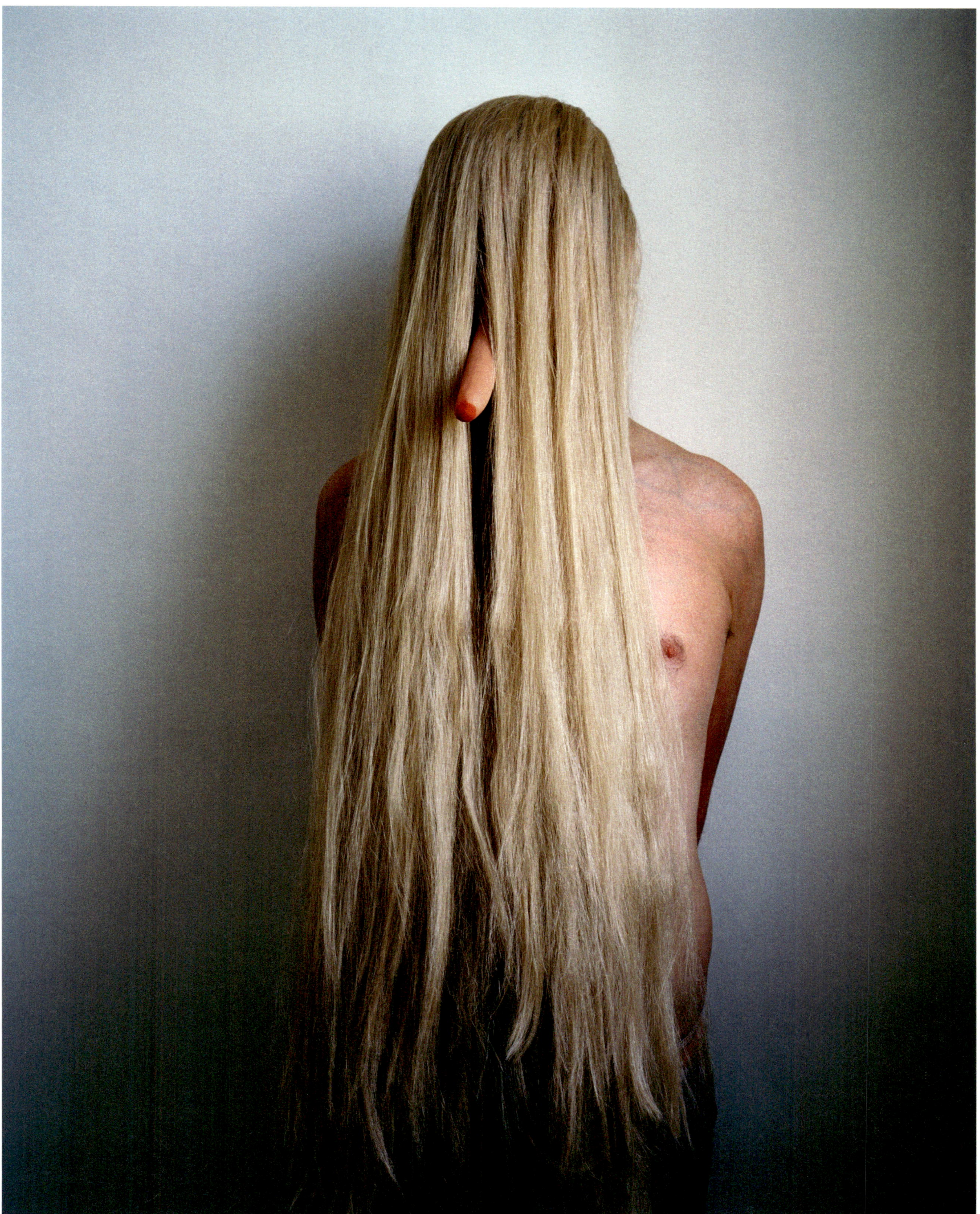

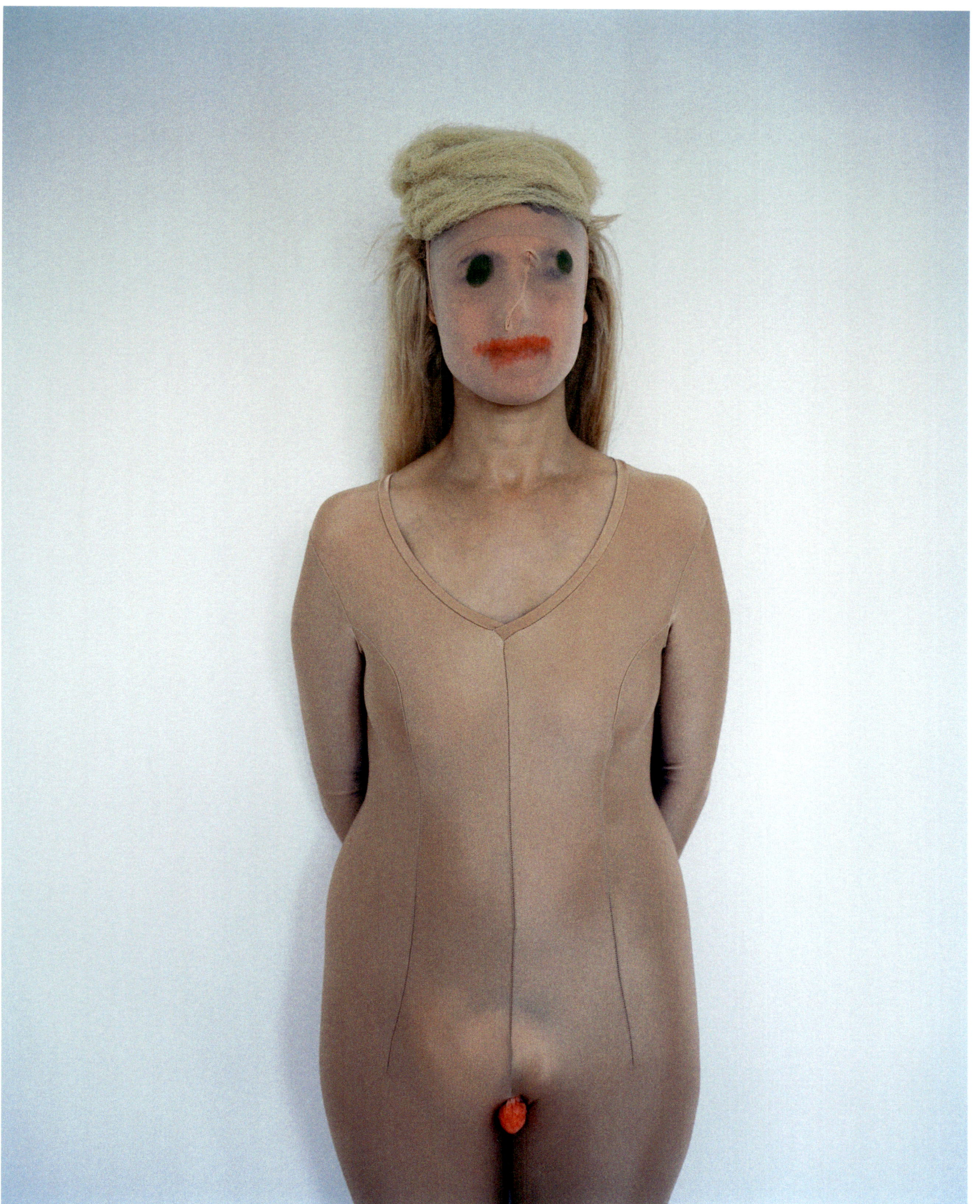

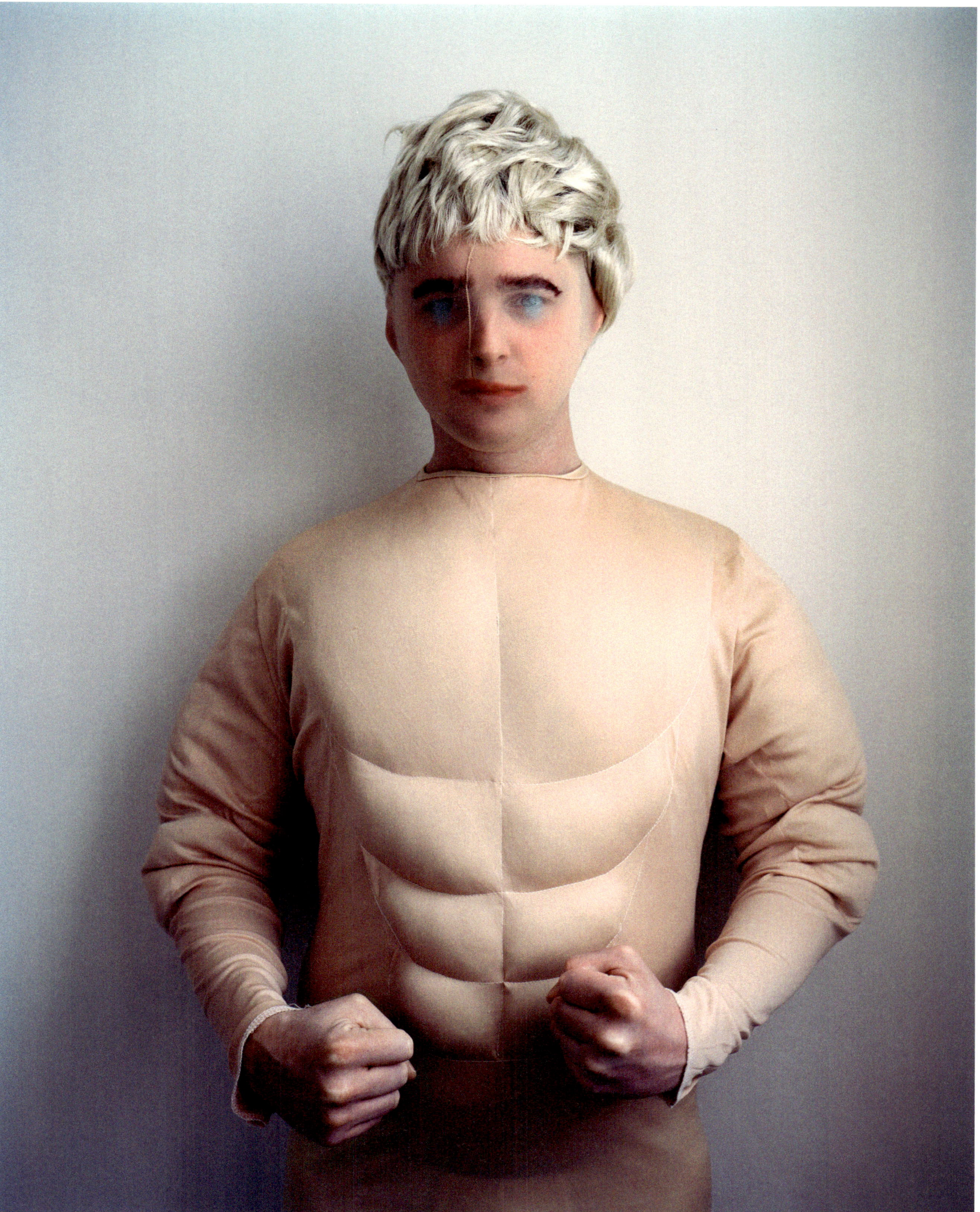

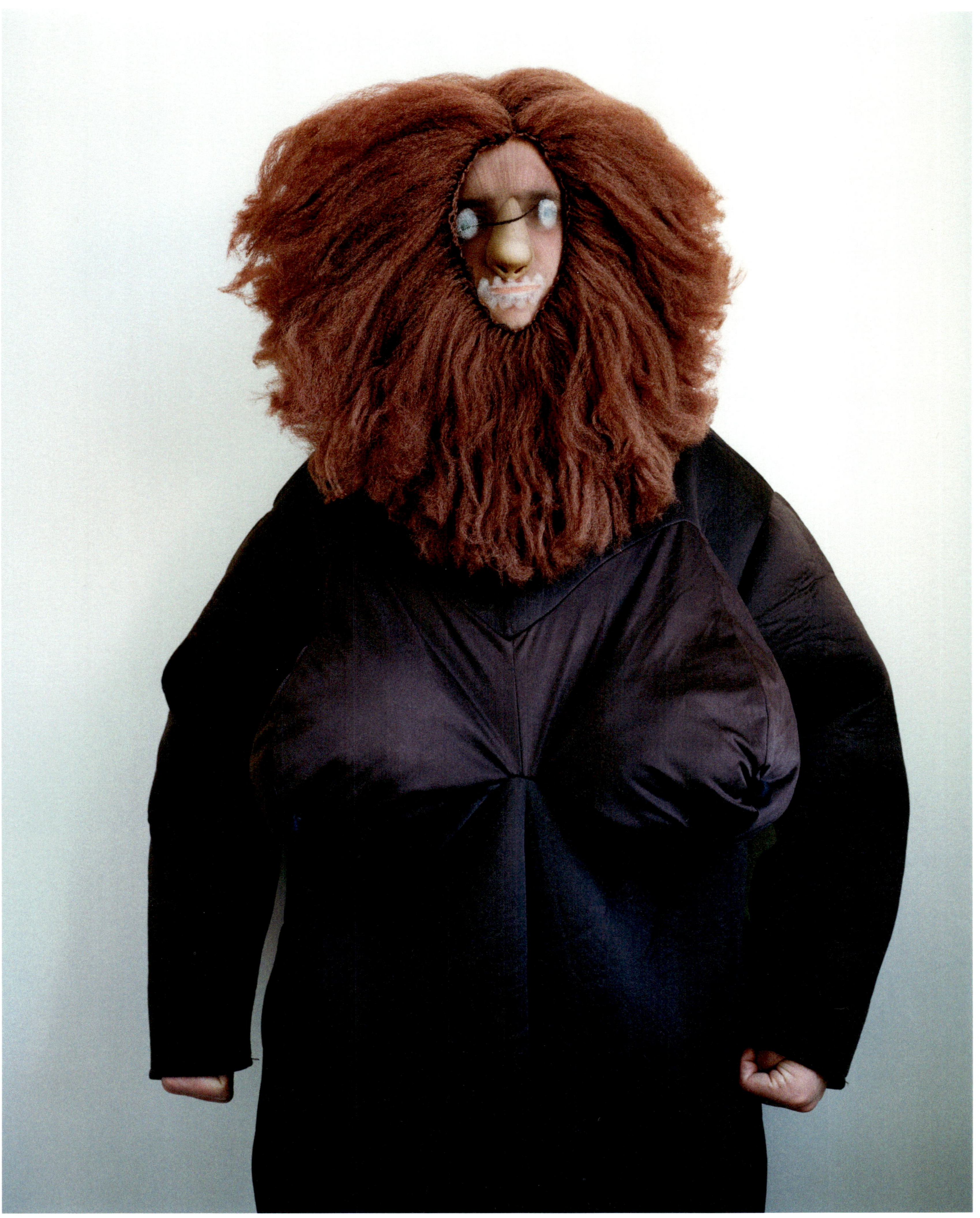

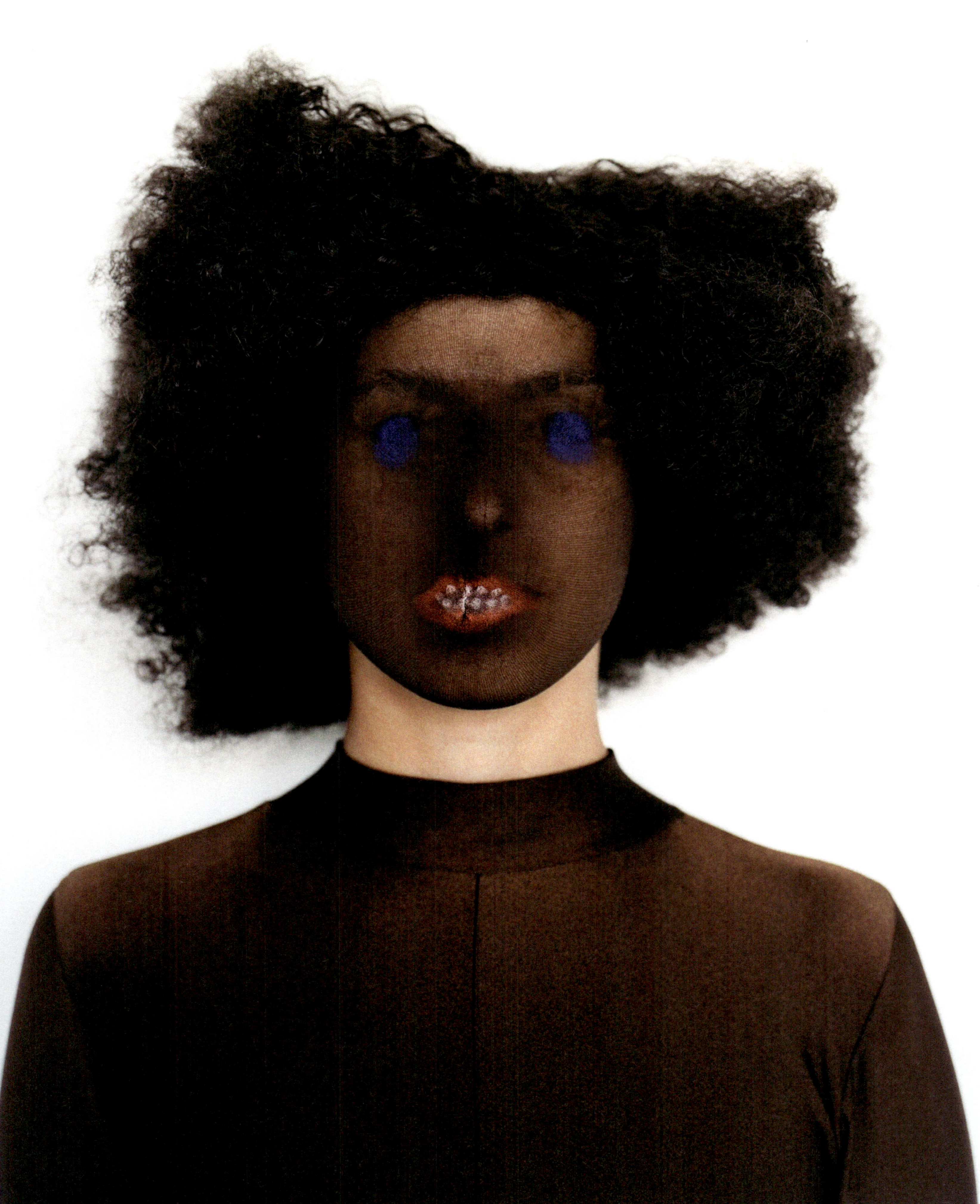

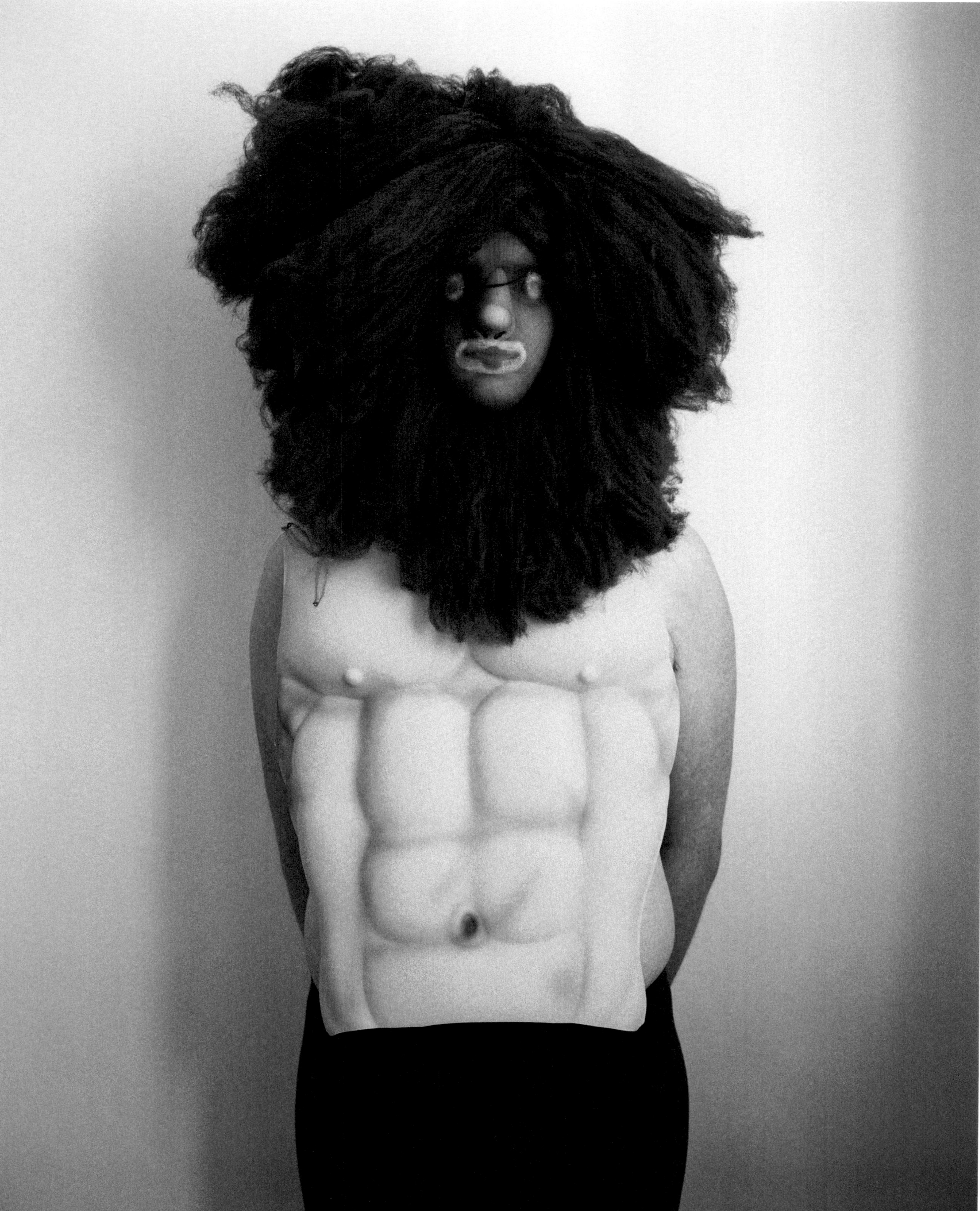

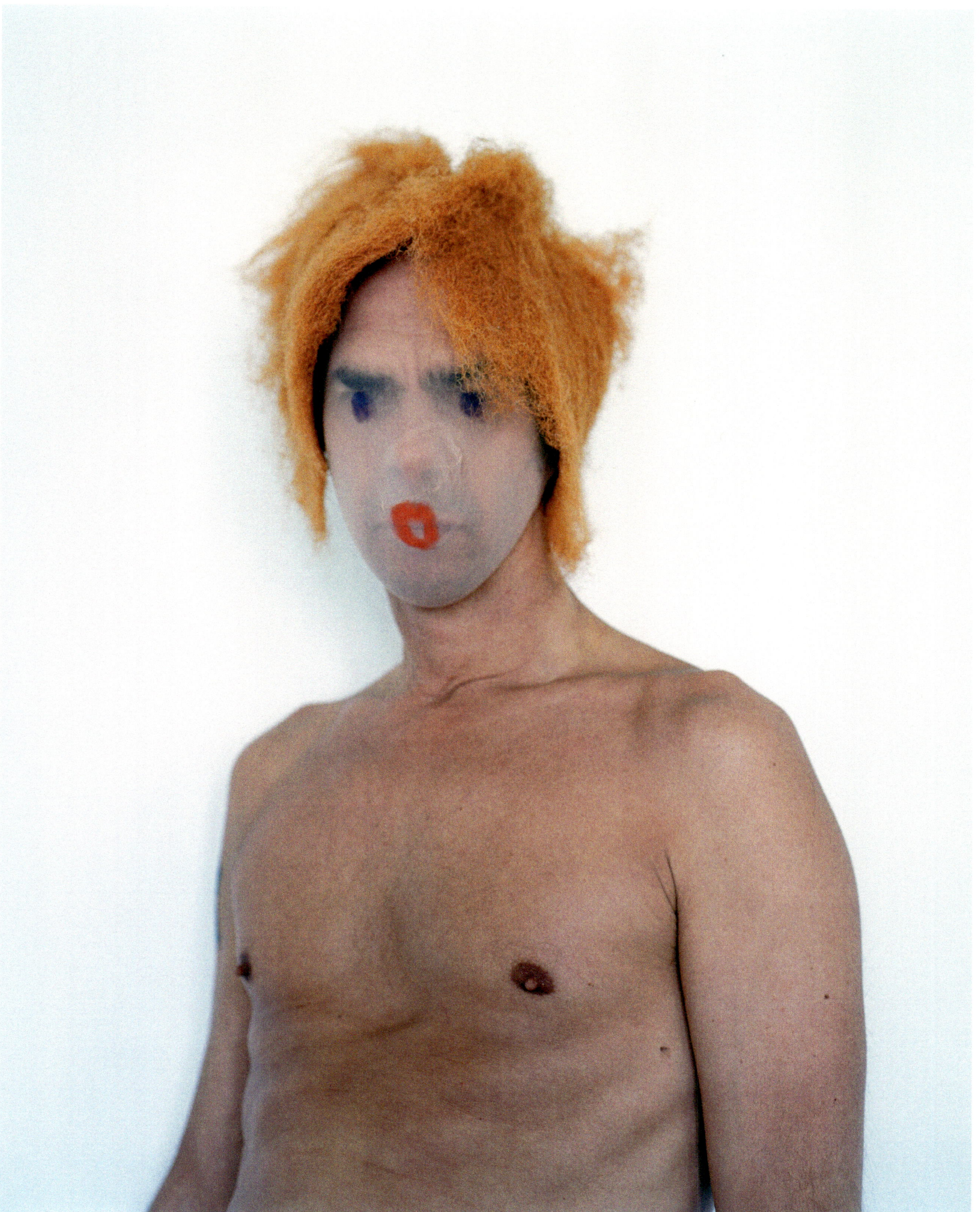

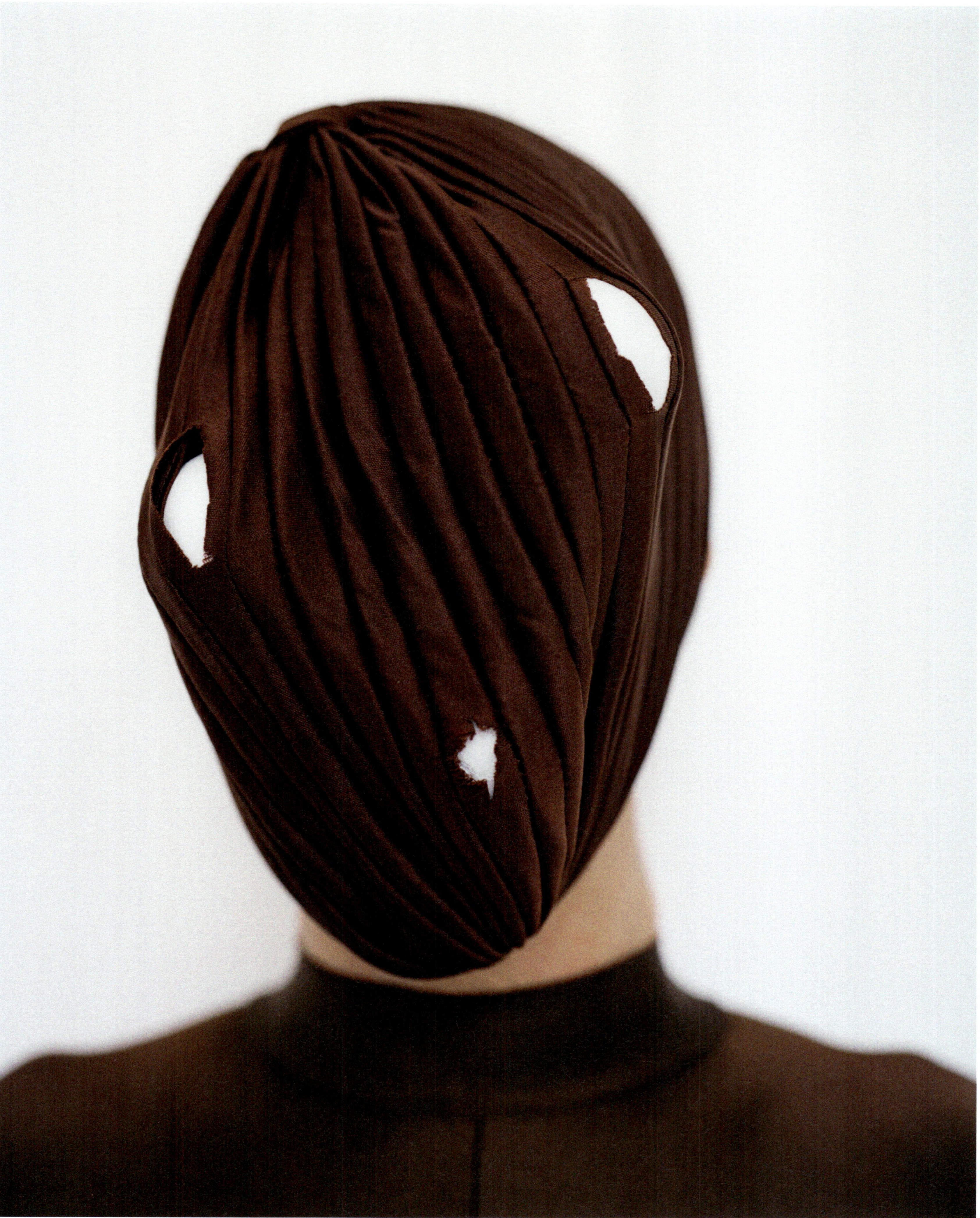

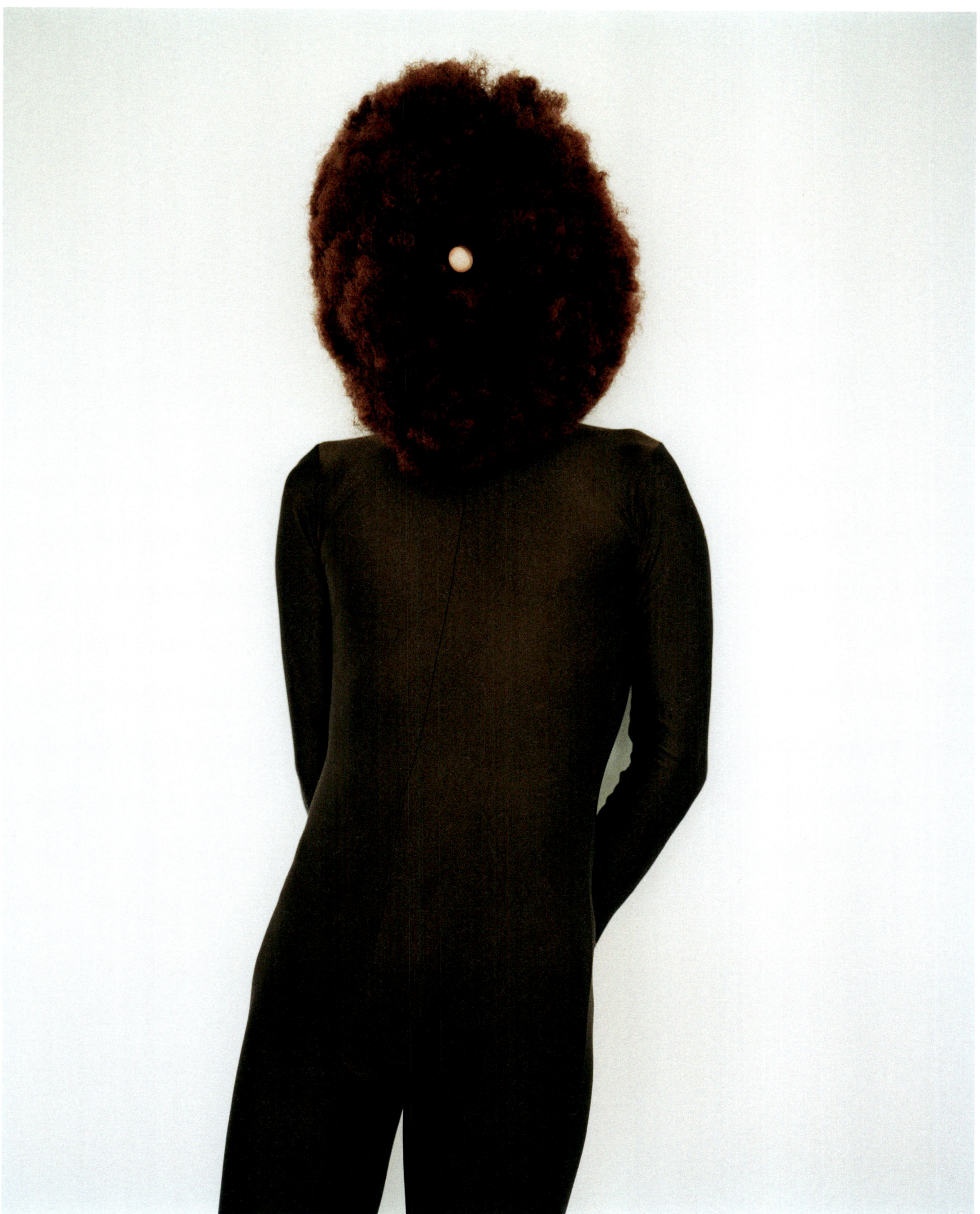

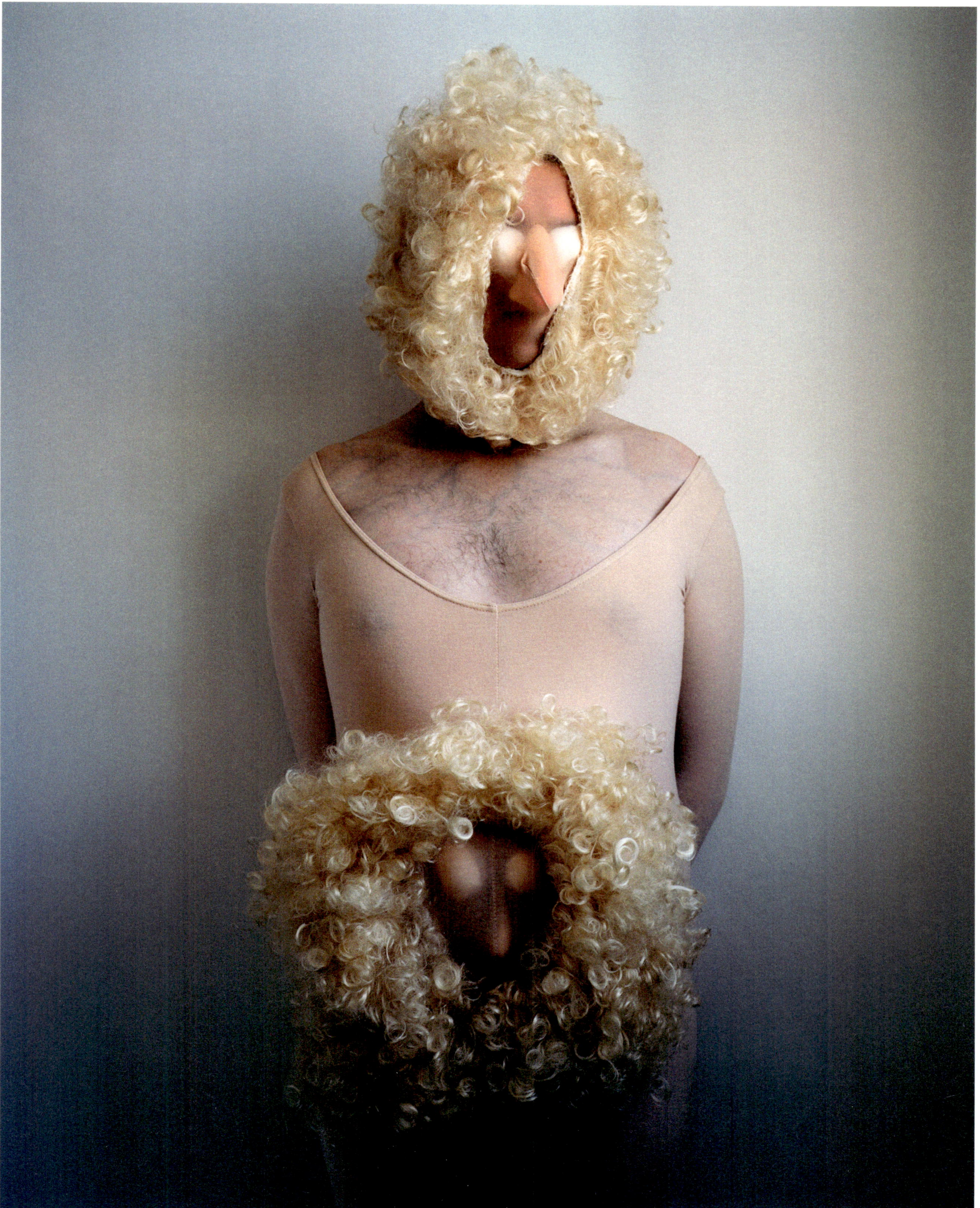

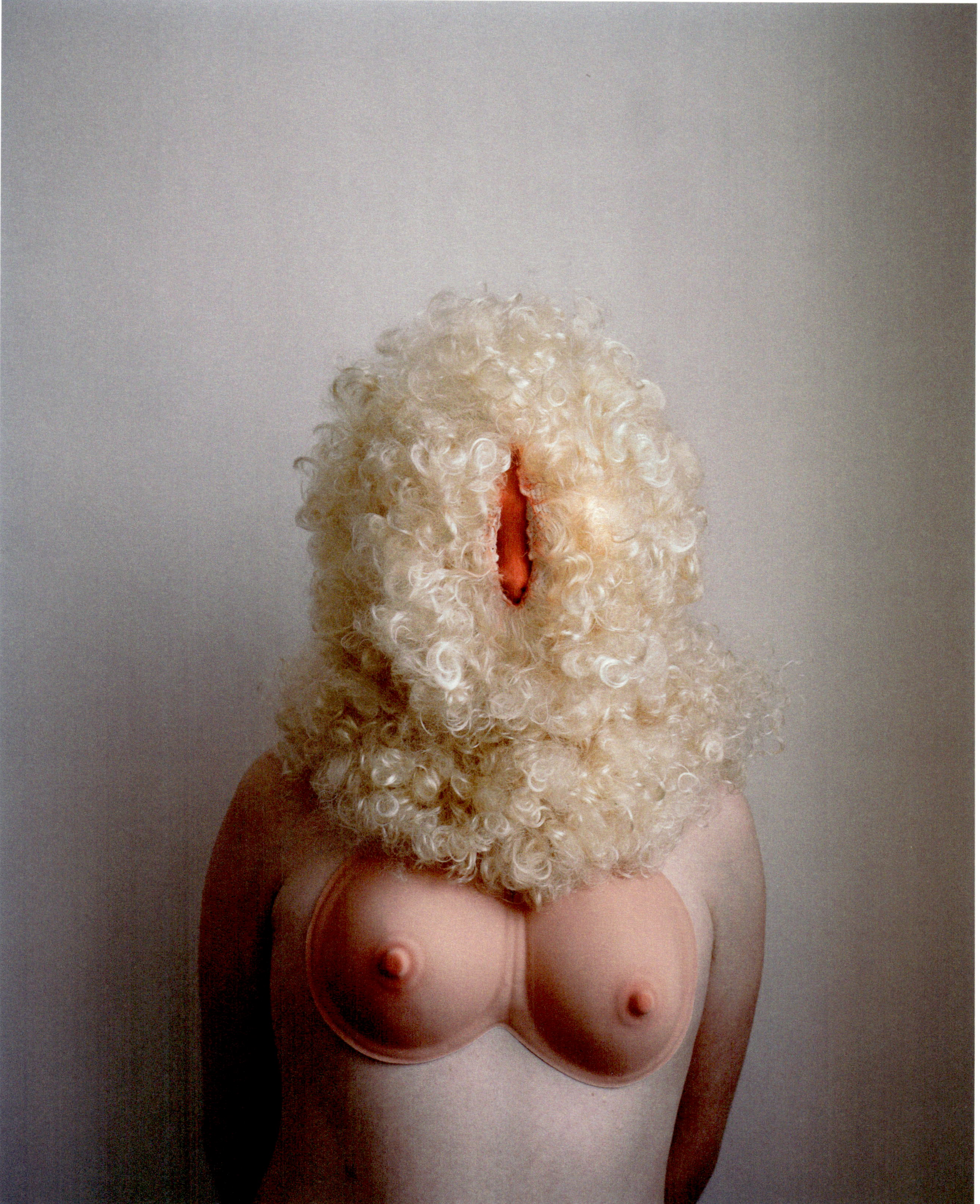

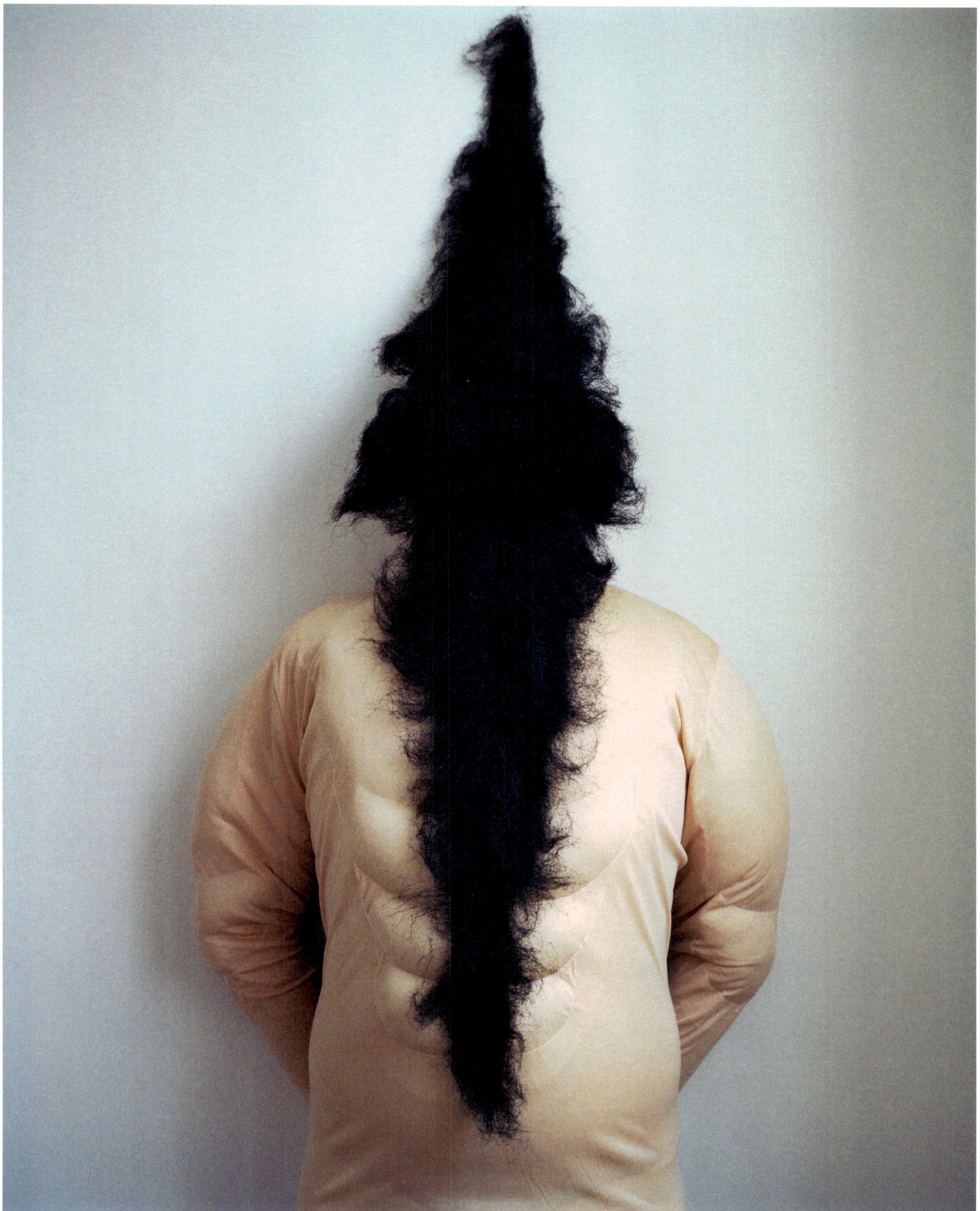

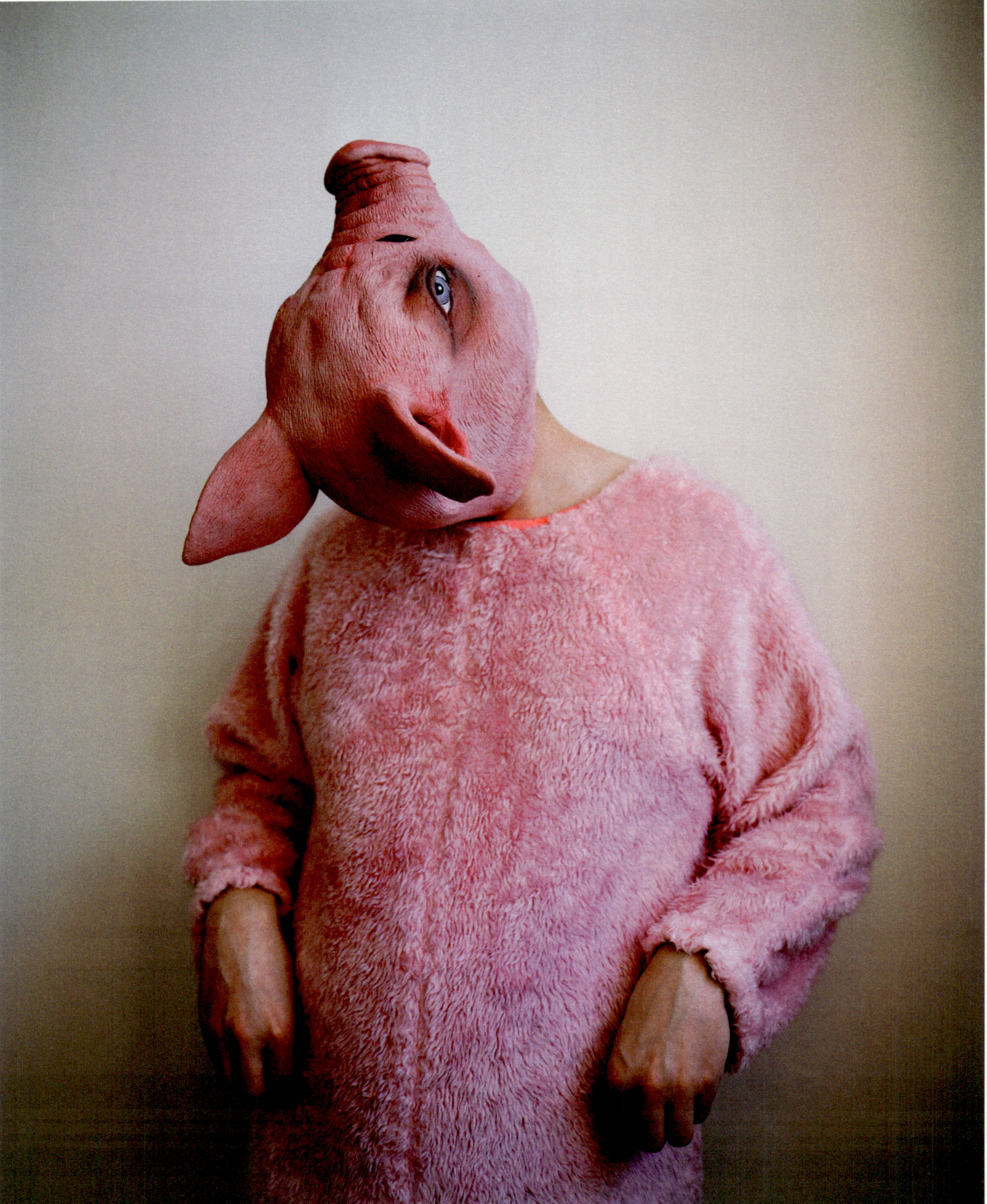

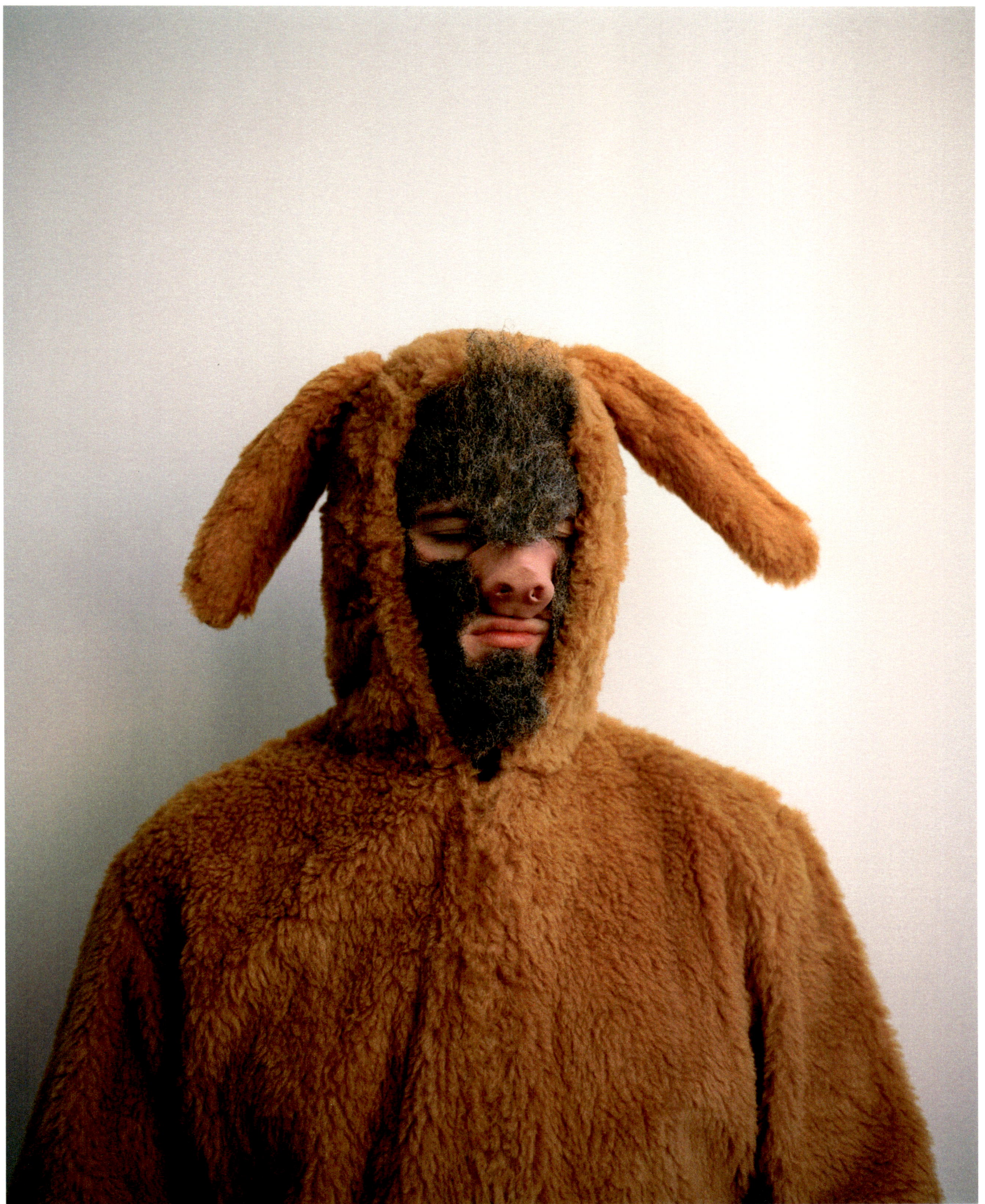

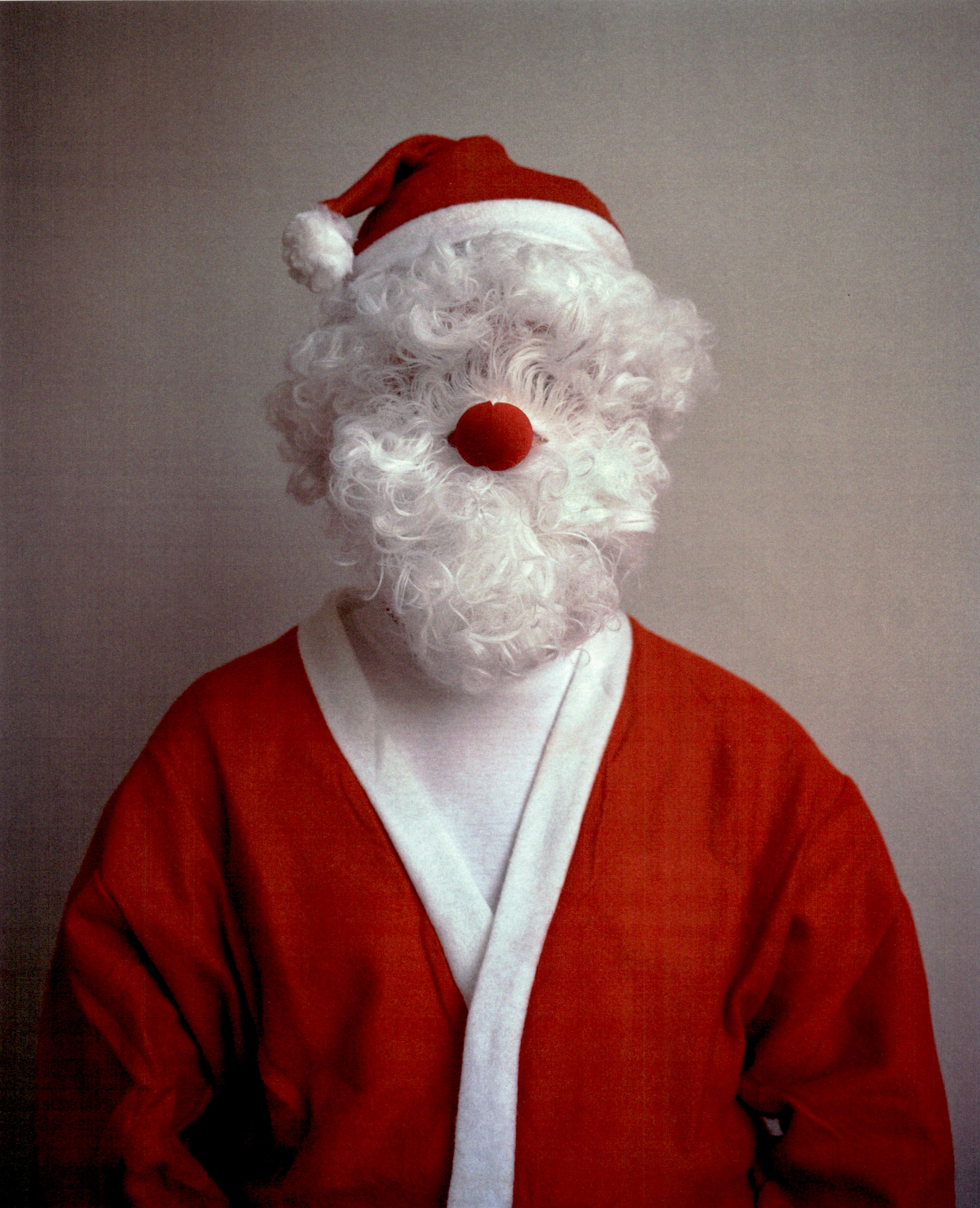

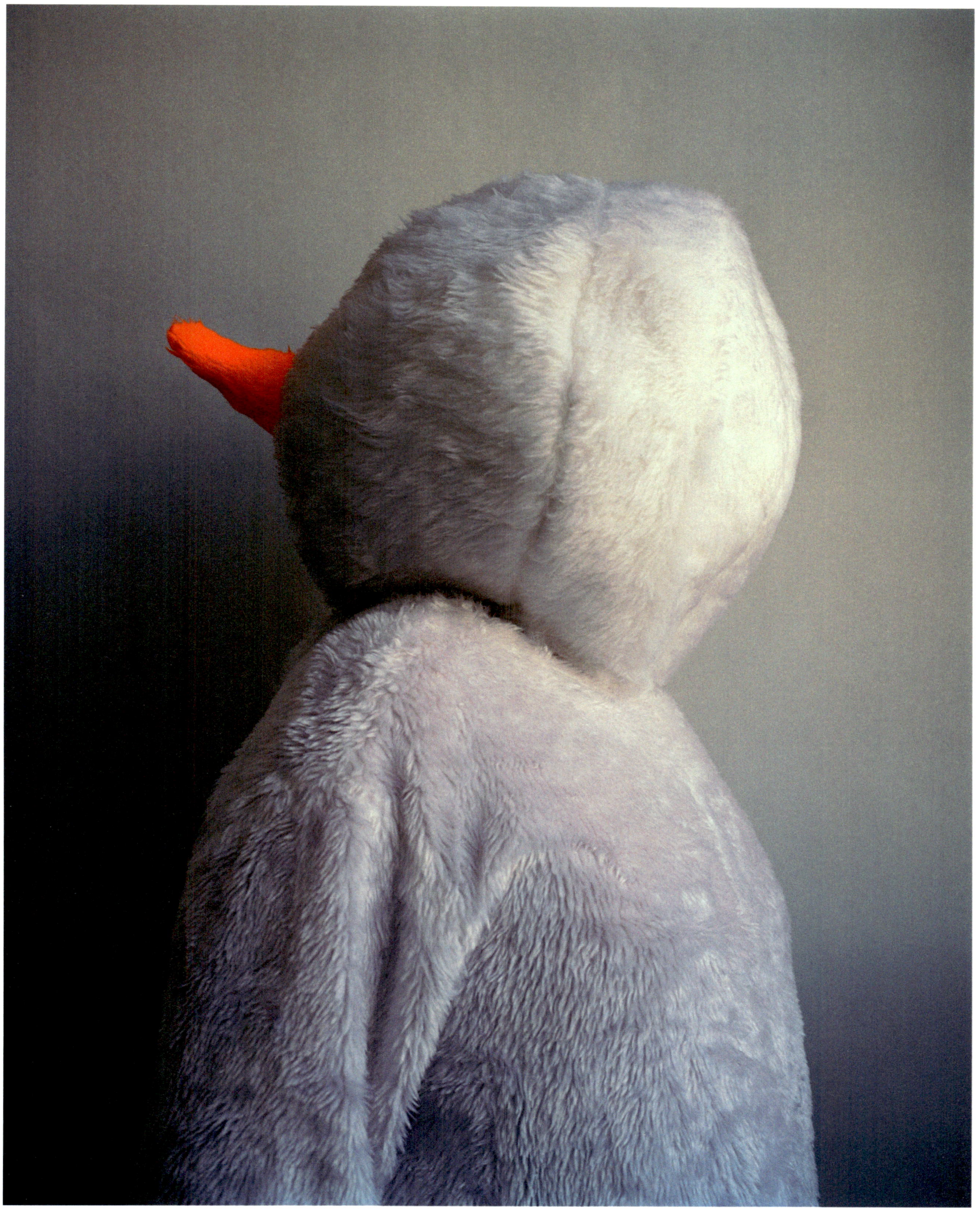

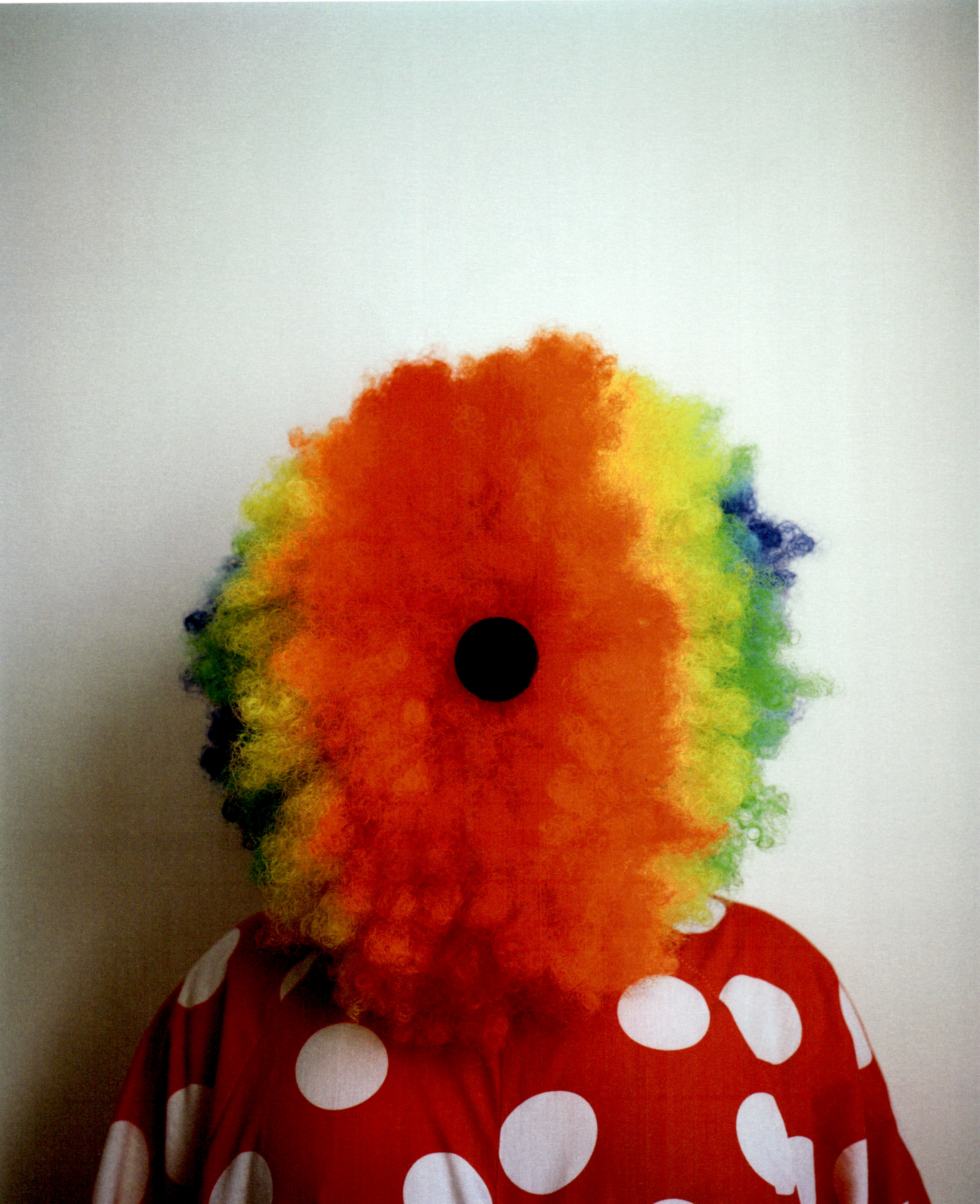

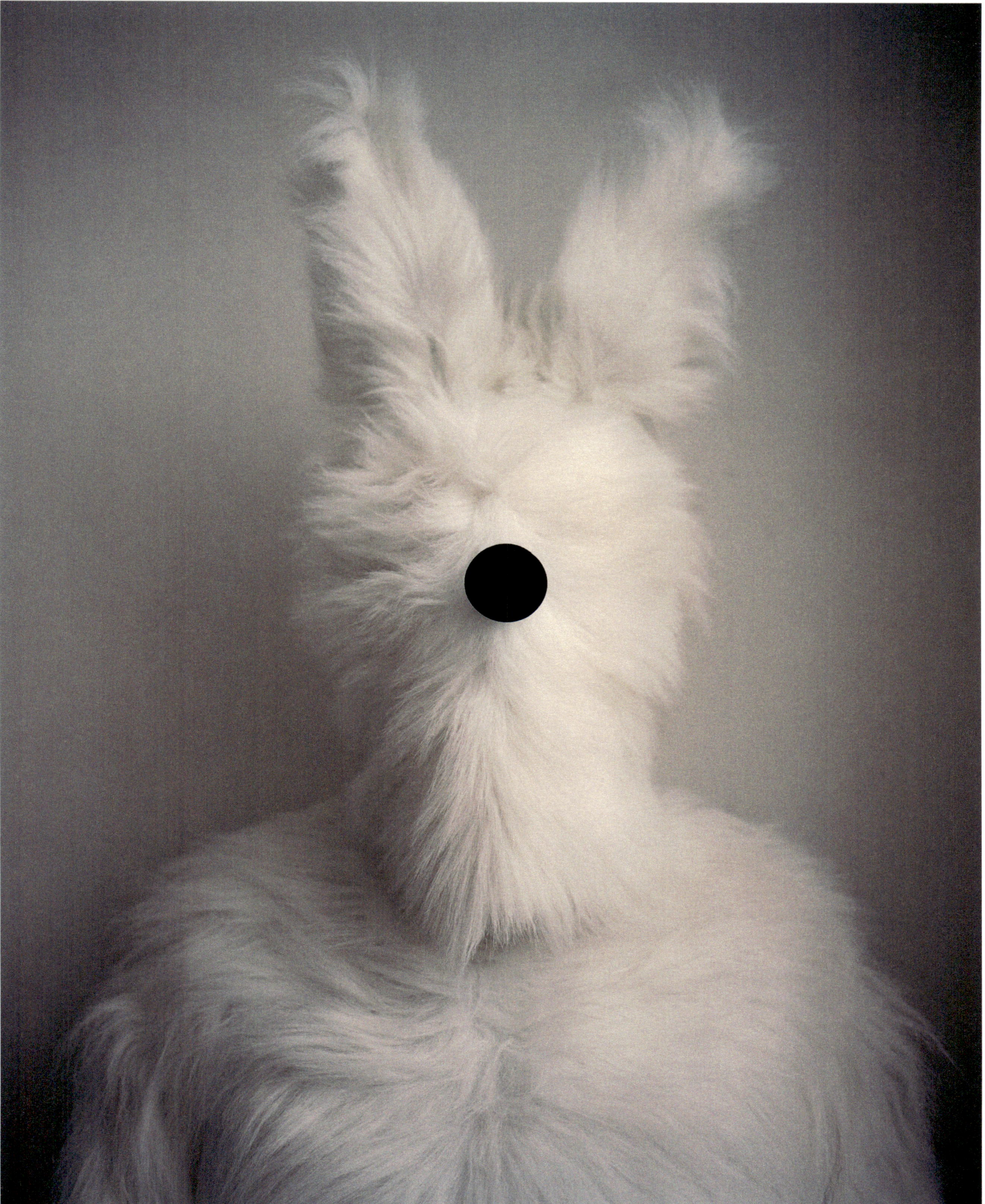

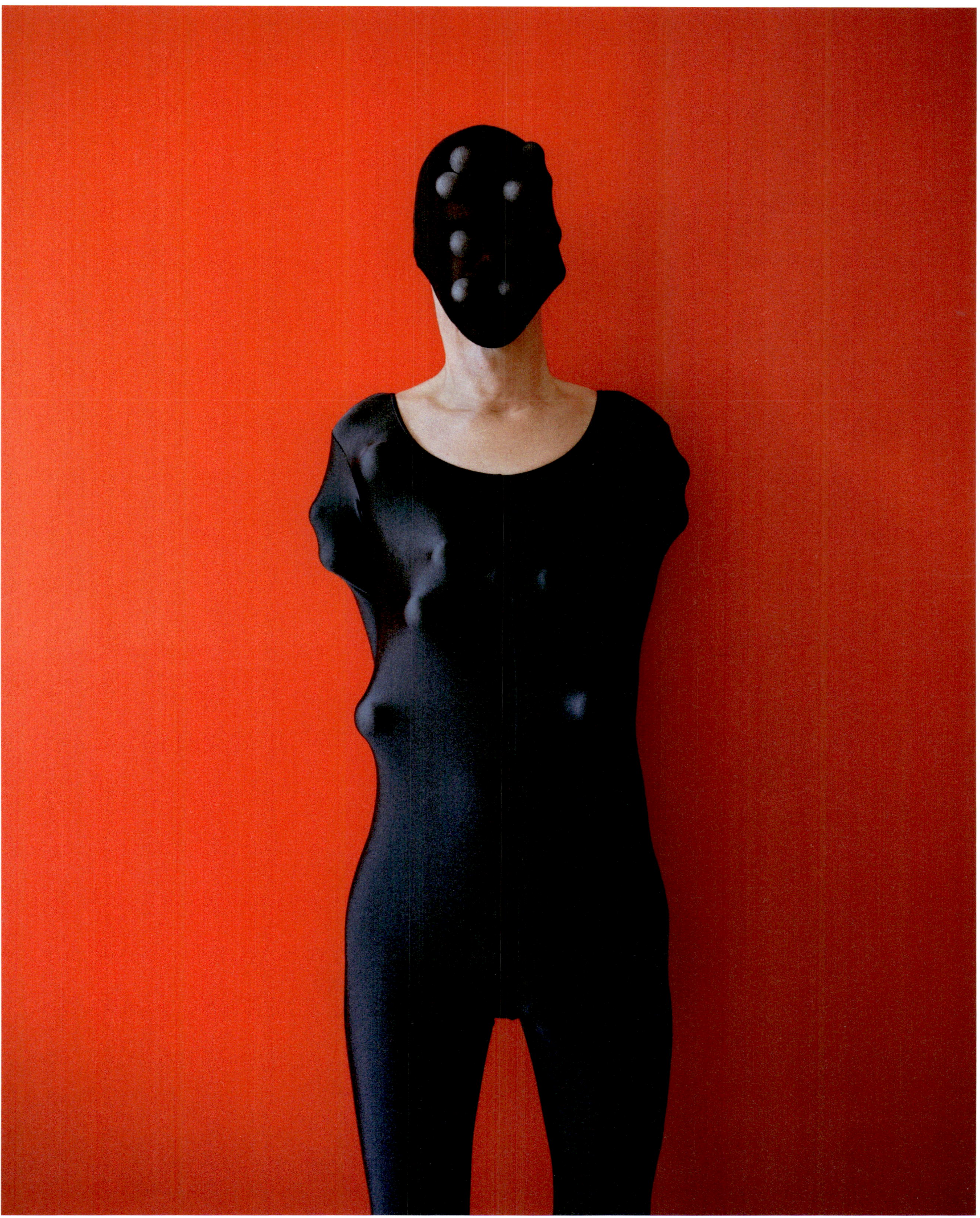

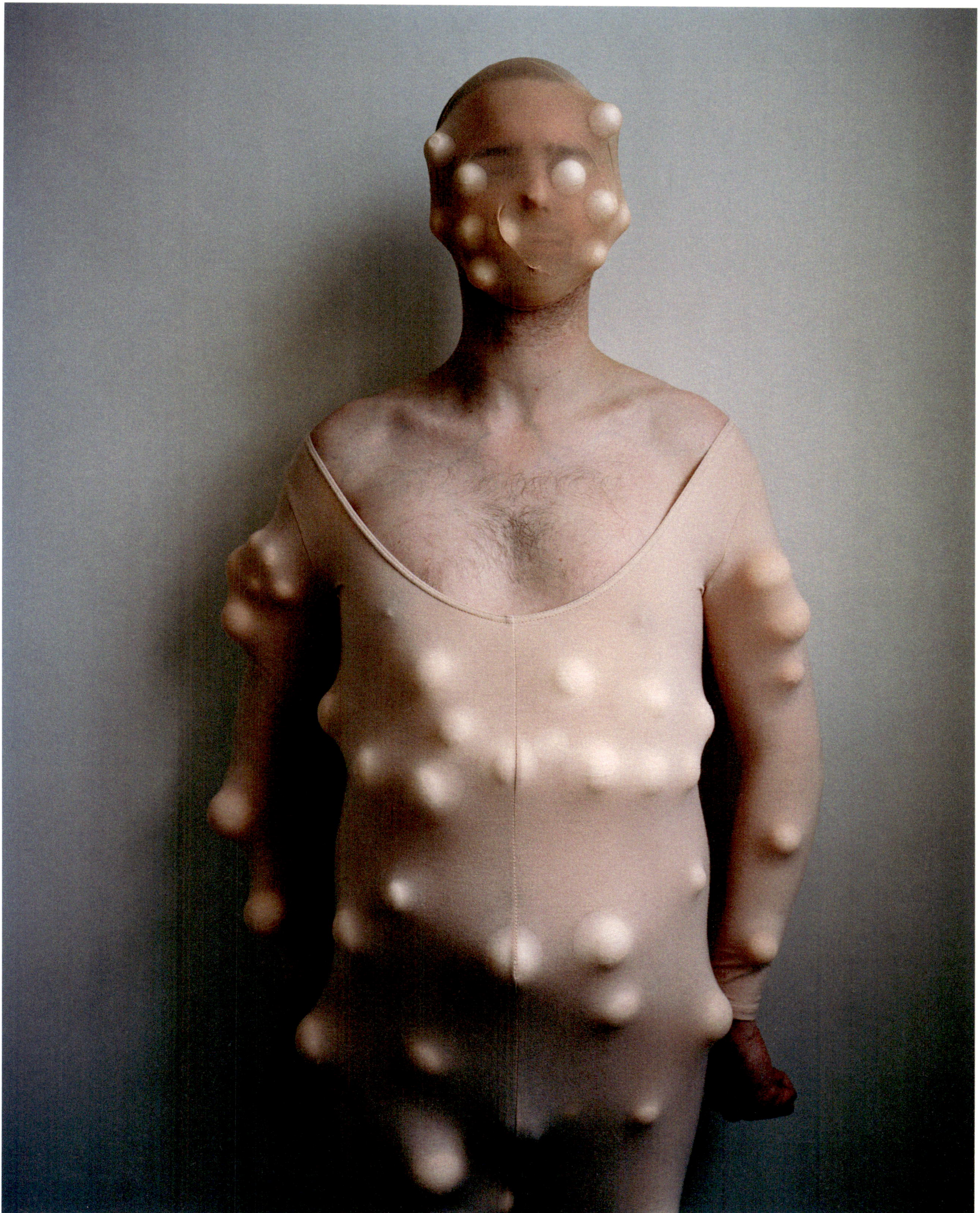

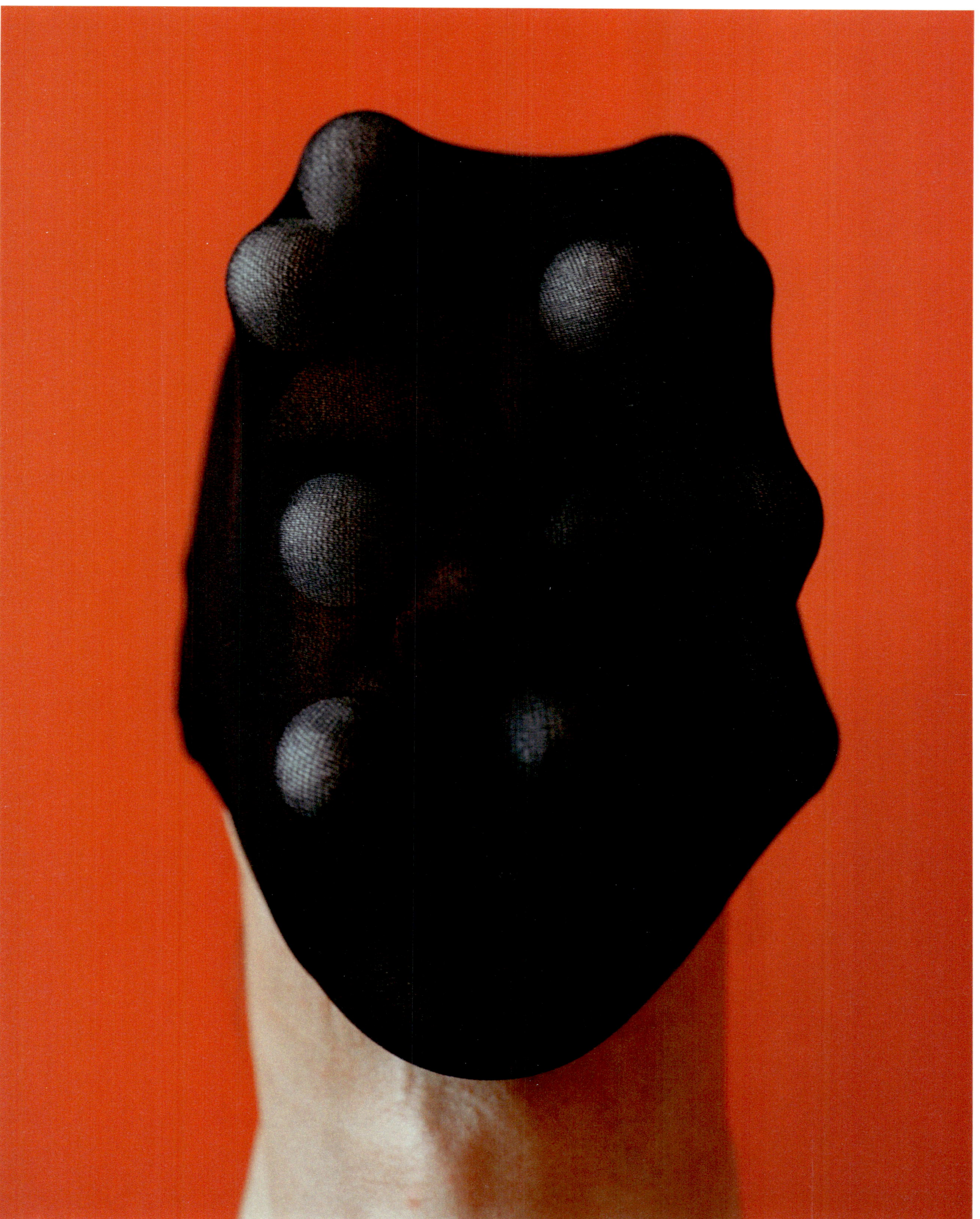

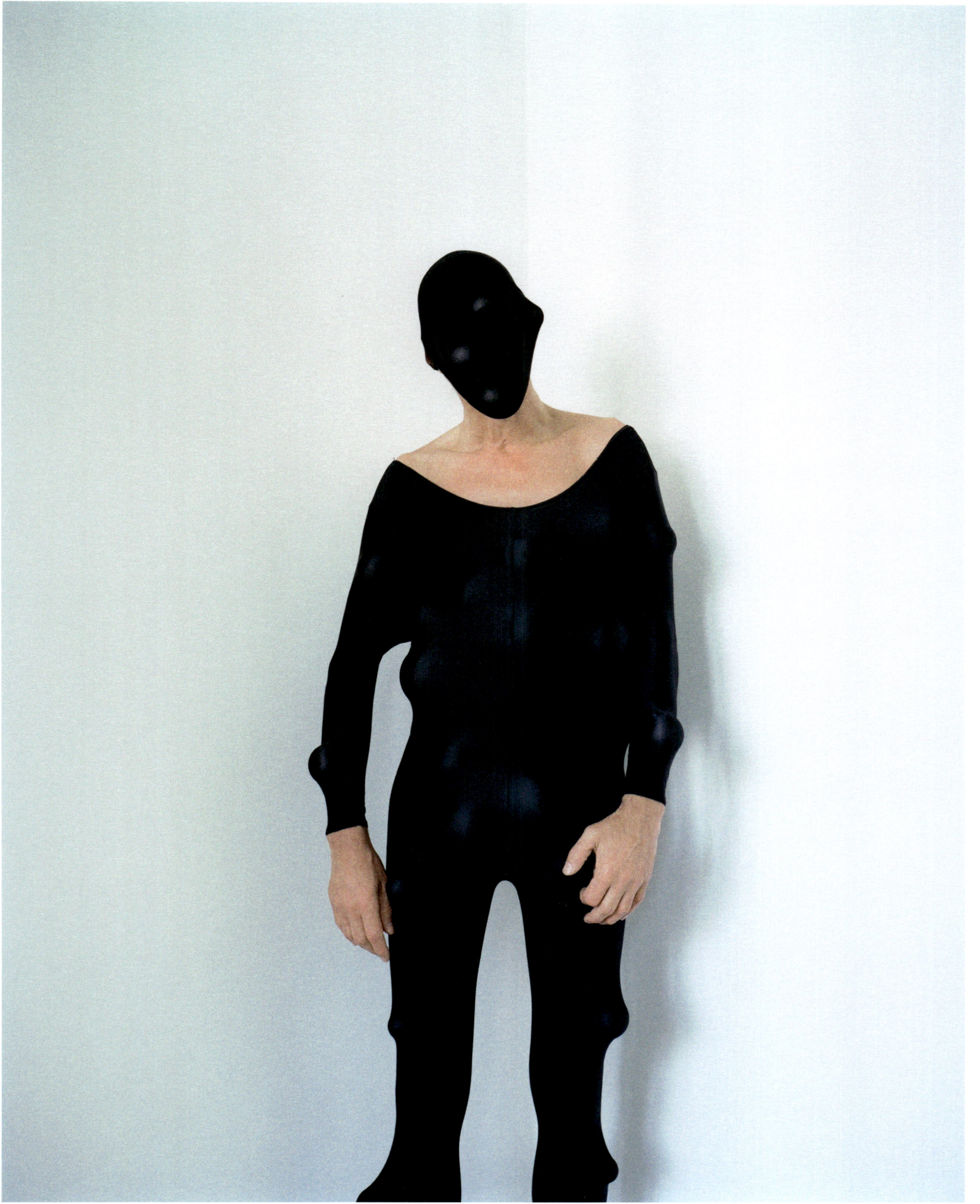

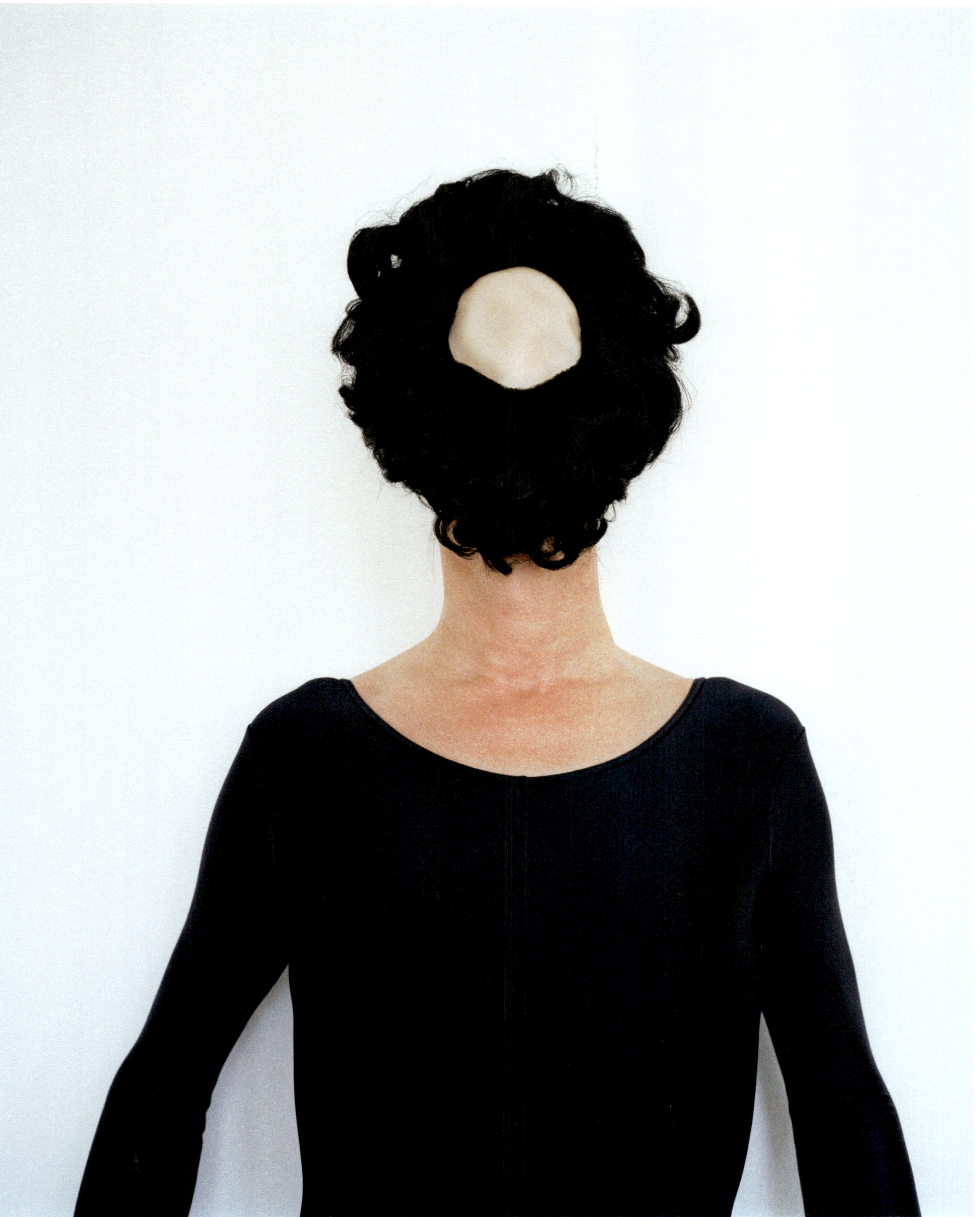

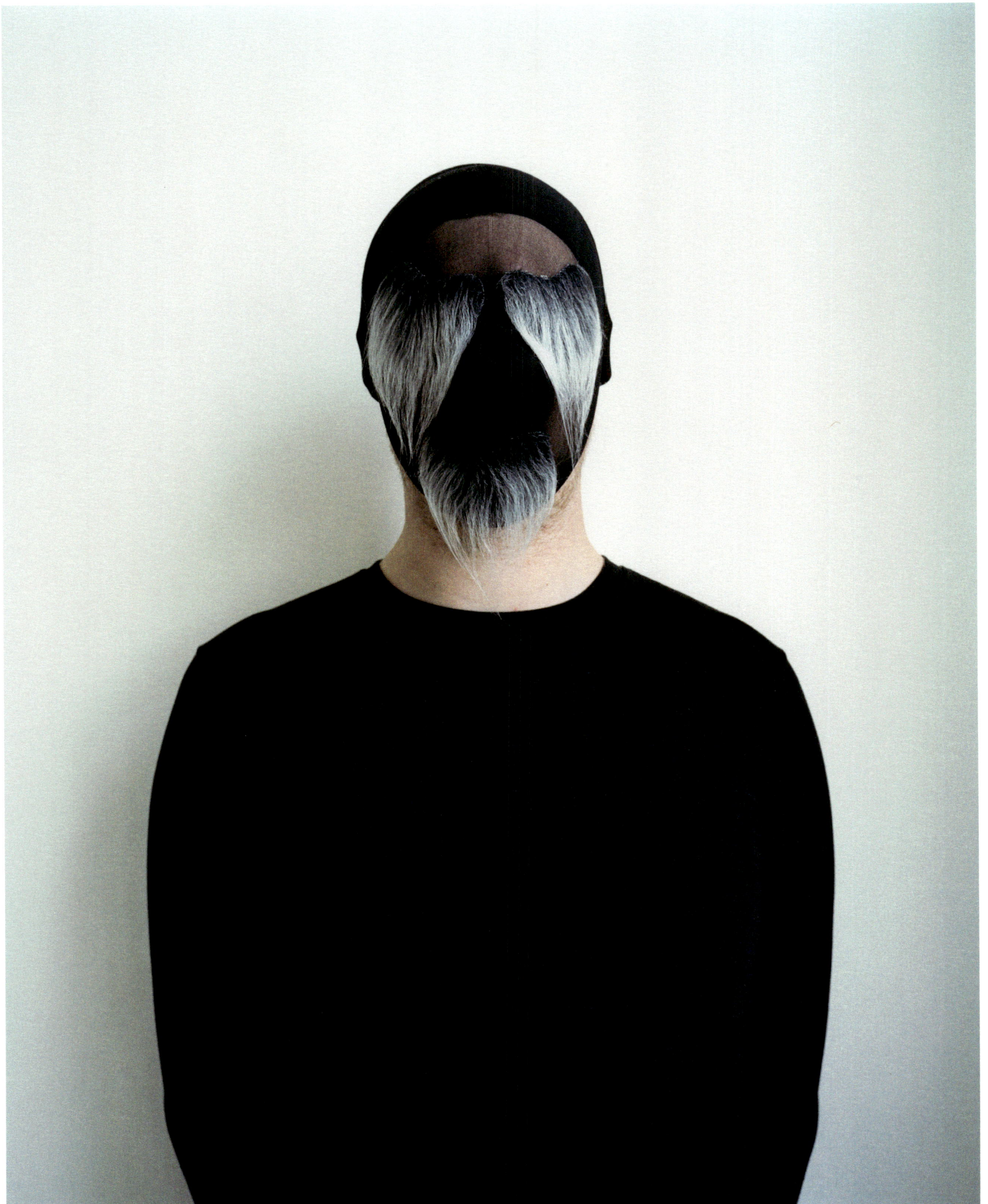

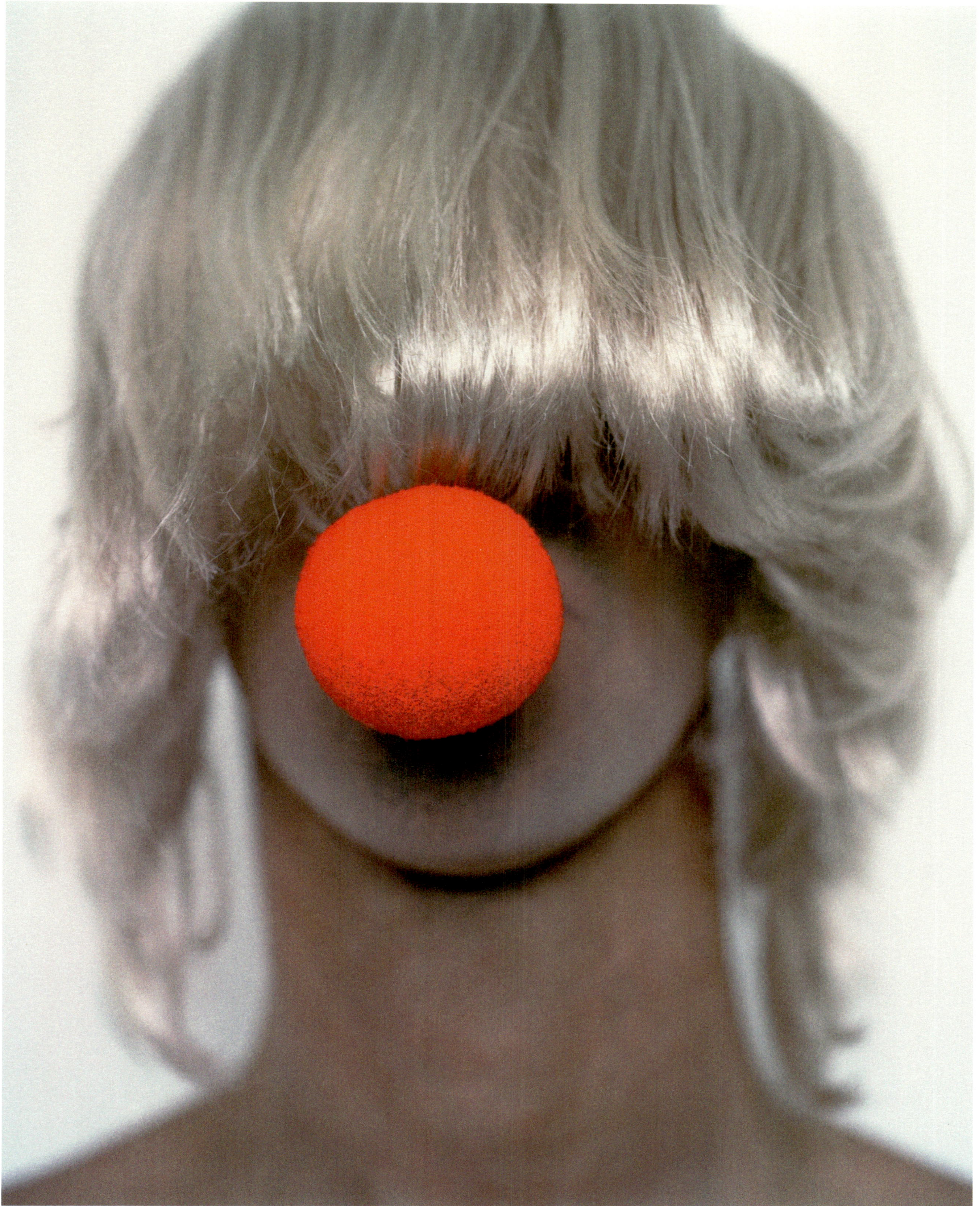

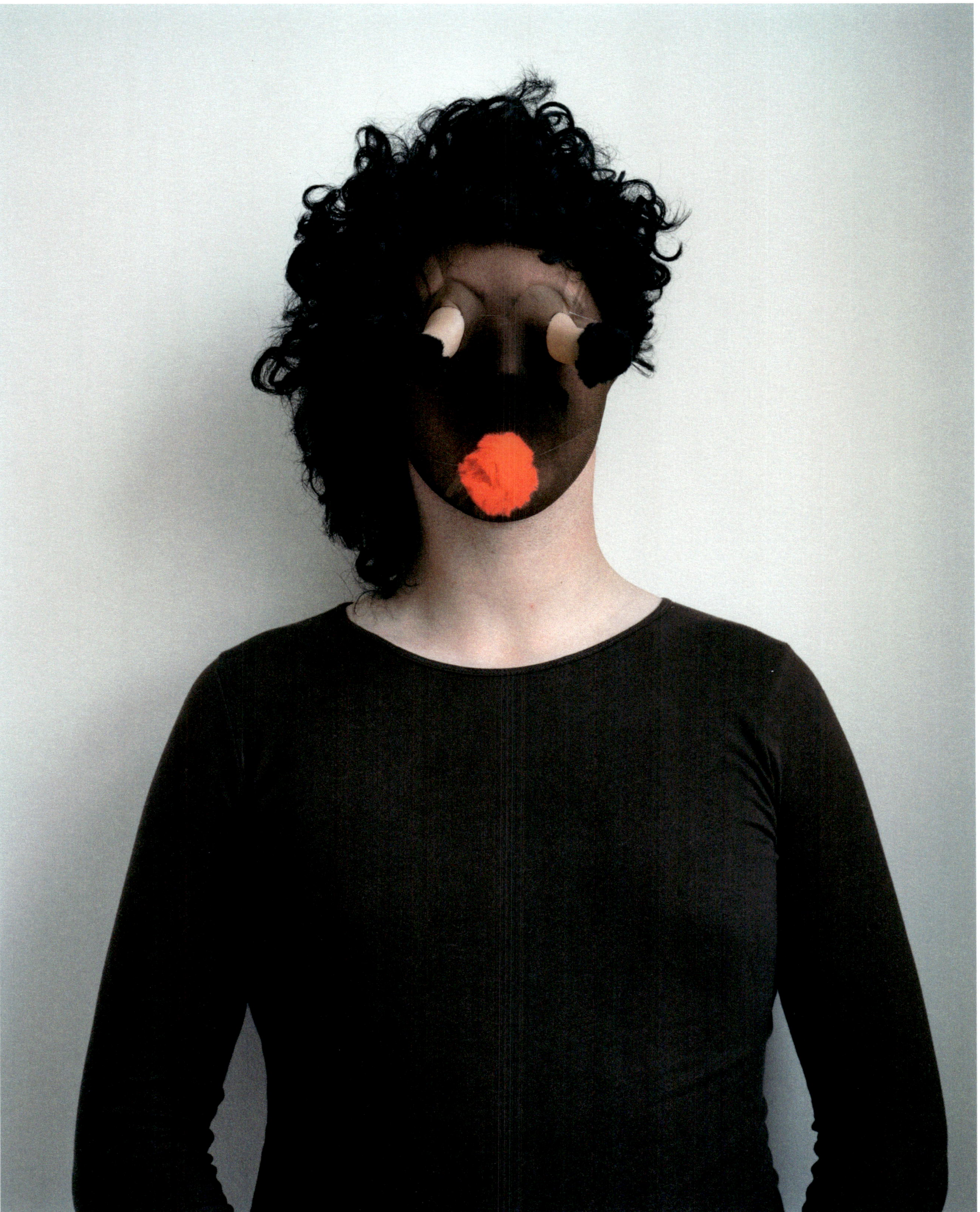

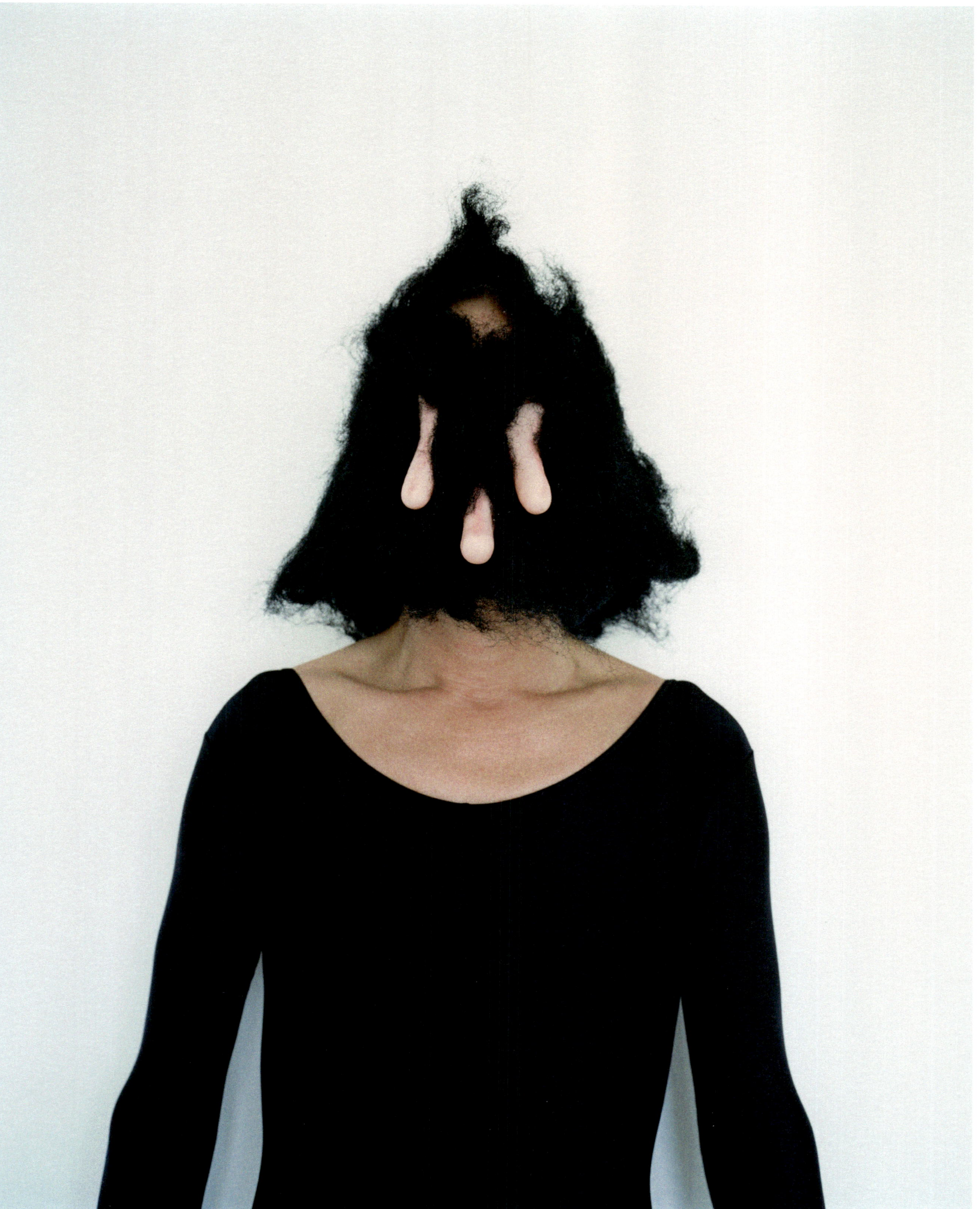

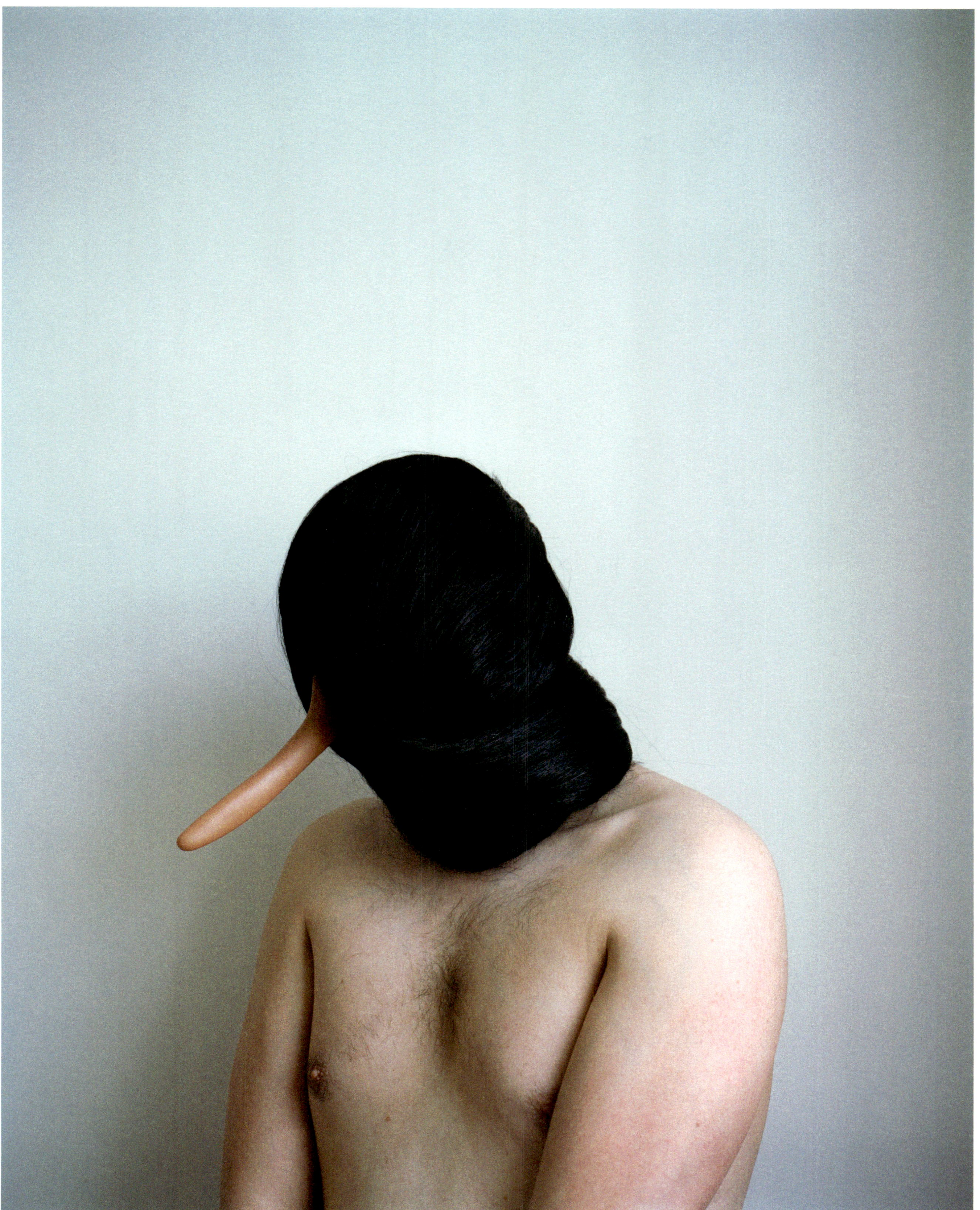

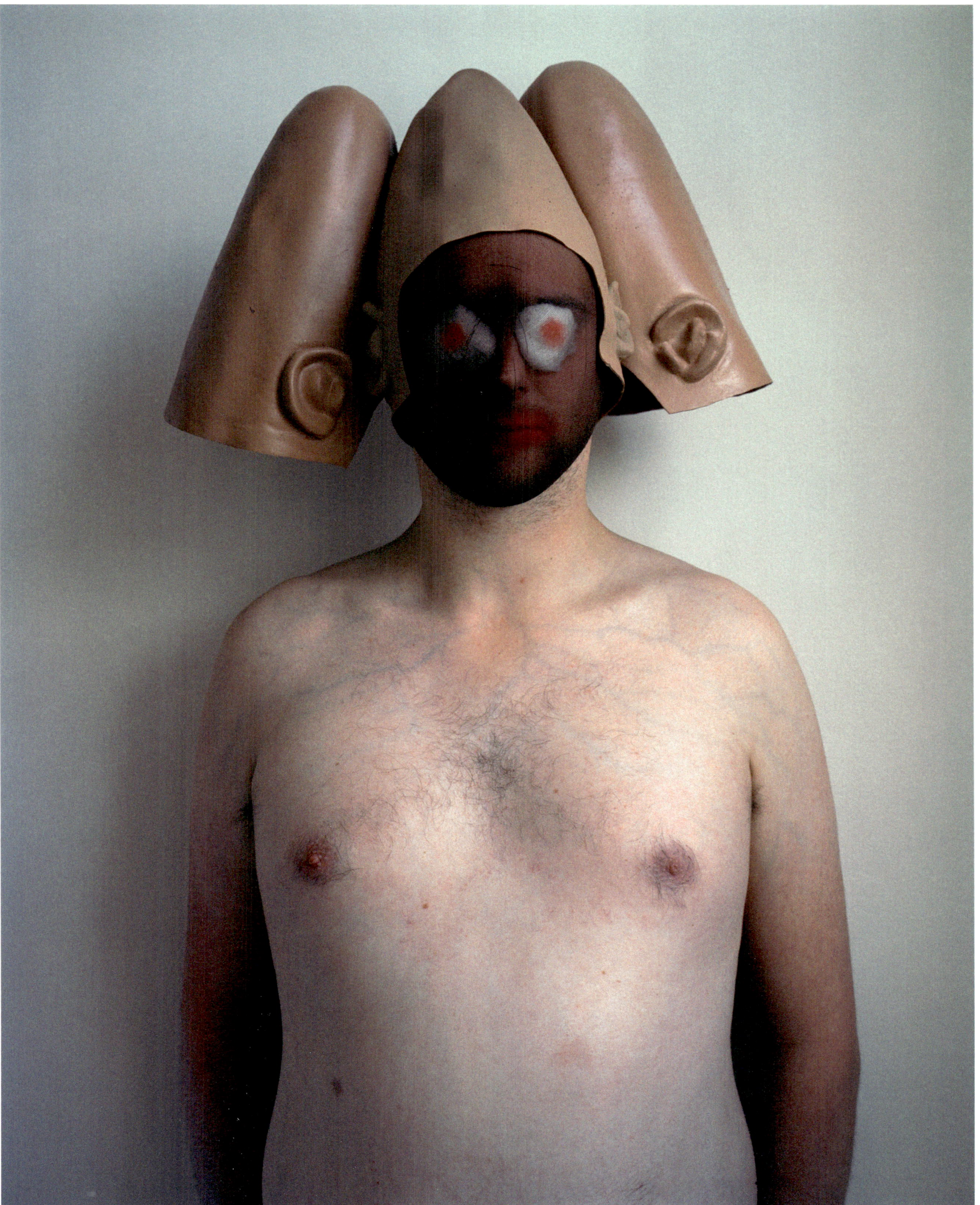

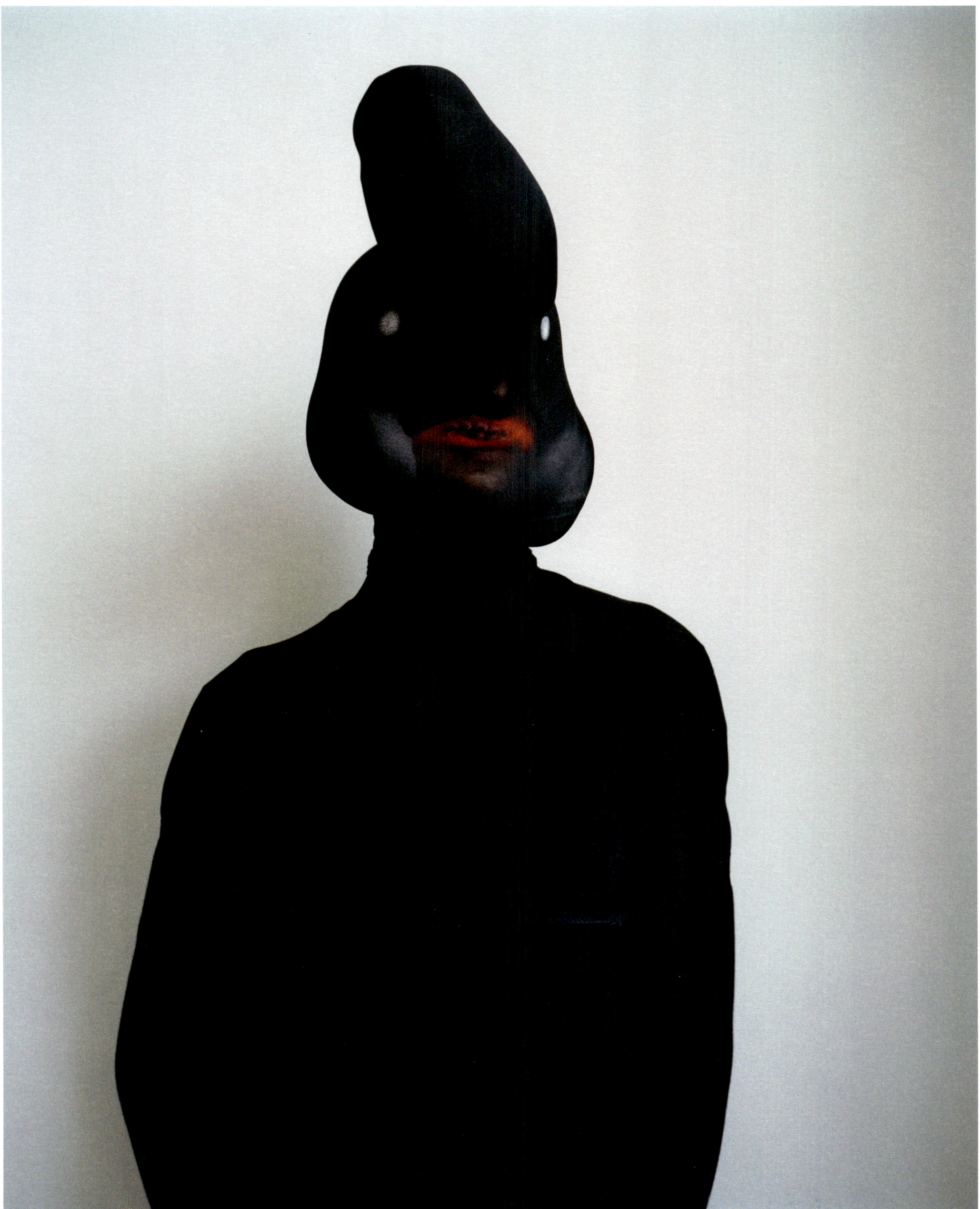

Thankyou to Mark Vessey,
Nick Cave, Sherald Lamden
and Ignacio Andreu
my friends and collaborators

Smudge

This book is published on the
occasion of the exhibition:
Polly Borland Smudge at
Gloria ActarBirkhäuser, Madrid

Publisher
Actar
Barcelona / New York
Part of ActarBirkhäuser
www.actar.com

Editor
Ignacio Andreu

Photo Digitalization
SpectrumPhoto
Thanks to Klair Bird,
Andy Ford and Paul Lowe

Graphic Design
Ramon Prat

Color Reproduction
Cromotex

Translation
Cillero & de Motta

Gloria
ActarBirkhäuser
C/ Hortaleza 116
28004 Madrid, Spain
info@abgloria.com
www.abgloria.com

Distribution
ActarBirkhäuserD
Barcelona – Basel – New York
www.actarbirkhauser-d.com

Roca i Batlle 2
E-08023 Barcelona
T +34 93 417 49 93
F +34 93 418 67 07
salesbarcelona@actarbirkhauser.com

Viaduktstrasse 42
CH-4051 Basel
T +41 61 5689 800
F +41 61 5689 899
salesbasel@actarbirkhauser.com

151 Grand Street, 5th Floor
New York, NY 10013
T +1 212 966 2207
F +1 212 966 2214
salesnewyork@actarbirkhauser.com

Polly Borland is represented in
Spain by Gloria ActarBirkhäuser
www.abgloria.com

Polly Borland is represented in
Australia by Murray White Room
www.murraywhiteroom.com

Polly Borland works
with Other Criteria in the UK
www.othercriteria.com

ISBN 978-84-92861-59-0
DL B-42294-2010

Printed and bound
in the European Union

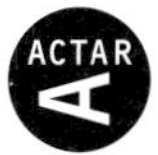

GLORIA